Reading Daphne

A guide to the writing of Daphne du Maurier for readers and book groups

Ella Westland

ISBN 978 185022 213 2

Published by Truran, Croft Prince, Mount Hawke,
Truro, Cornwall TR4 8EE
www.truranbooks.co.uk

Truran is an imprint of Truran Books Ltd

Printed and bound in Cornwall by R. Booth Ltd,
Antron Hill, Mabe, Penryn, TR10 9HH

For Anna

Contents

PART 3 THREE TALES OF TERROR

PART 4 IT'S ONLY THE SISTER

PART 5 EAST WIND

Preface

One hundred years ago, on 13 May 1907, Daphne du Maurier was born into a gifted family in London. Her father Gerald was a fêted actor and theatre manager; her grandfather George, the creator of Trilby and Svengali, had been a celebrated writer and *Punch* cartoonist. Daphne had a lot to live up to, but she was determined to forge her own career as an author – and in that ambition she was to succeed magnificently. Her parents might have expected their daughter to inherit some kind of artistic talent, but they could not have predicted that a century later the name of Daphne du Maurier would outshine them all.

Her reputation has enjoyed a surge of interest since her death in 1989, and the unspoilt coastal region around Fowey in Cornwall has become 'du Maurier Country'. Annual festivals have been held there every May since 1997, bringing hundreds of fans to Cornwall to enjoy a week of talks, walks, music and books at the height of the bluebell season.

Daphne's renewed popularity has spread far beyond Fowey, and her writing is treated more seriously than it has ever been. A website has been set up for fans to exchange views on their reading. Her work is discussed in academic publications and seminar rooms from North America to Australia. The University of Exeter has set up substantial archives with material on loan from the du Maurier family, where you can read George du Maurier's notebook or track the changes made to the typescript of *Rebecca*. Attractive new editions of her work published by Virago include new essays by novelists and critics who acknowledge her continuing influence in the twenty-first century. Nearly two decades of fresh enthusiasm for Daphne du Maurier's writing culminate in the centenary celebrations of 2007, which provide a unique occasion for revaluing her achievement.

Reading Daphne invites you inside the enthralling world of Daphne's imagination. It takes the unusual approach of providing commentaries on extracts from her work, in addition to discussing the best-known novels in depth. Members of book clubs may want to make use of it in their meetings. But if you are, like most readers, snatching time at home to enjoy Daphne du Maurier's thrilling fiction in solitude, having this guide beside you will encourage you to become a more adventurous reader.

How to Use This Book

PART 1 discusses eight important themes in Daphne's writing. You do not have to cover them all. You can pick out the ones that interest you most, and find out more about her early heroines or haunted houses, her love of Cornwall or lifelong fascination with Peter Pan. All the extracts you need are provided for you.

PART 2 takes a fresh look at five of her greatest novels. You may decide to select one or two of them, perhaps re-reading *Rebecca* or immersing yourself for the first time in *The Flight of the Falcon*. **Read the book first**, and keep a reading diary to make a few notes of your own before comparing your ideas with the guide.

PART 3 tempts you to read more of Daphne's short stories.

PART 4 introduces the writing of her sister, Angela du Maurier.

PART 5 gives you the chance to read a story, previously unpublished in the UK, written when the author was 19.

The guide ends with recommendations for places to visit and books to read, so that you can pursue your own interests in Daphne's life and writing.

Recommended Editions

Most of Daphne du Maurier's books have been reprinted in the new Virago series with introductions by writers and critics.

It's Only the Sister, Angela du Maurier's sparkling autobiography, and two of Angela's best novels, have been reprinted by Truran Books.

Page numbers refer to the editions listed in the section *Reading On* p.167

BOOK GROUPS

a suggested schedule

1st meeting – each reader in the group introduces an important theme using the extracts provided in Part 1.

2nd meeting – one novel is chosen from Part 2 to read in advance. One member of the group reads the related chapter in the guide and provides a summary for discussion.

Other ideas – watch the Hitchcock film of *Rebecca*, read one of Angela du Maurier's books, compare two short stories, or ask each reader to introduce a striking episode from Daphne's work.

HOME ALONE

Reading is, ultimately, an intensely private activity, but you can use this book to stimulate your own ideas.

Keep a reading diary, and record your impressions for yourself. Or find a friend who enjoys the same kind of books, and read alongside each other for a few weeks.

Never be afraid to challenge the point of view expressed in the following pages! Your diary should be a dialogue with this guide that develops your own understanding of Daphne du Maurier's imagination.

Introduction
a writer's life

The turning point of Daphne du Maurier's life was the day she began her first novel. Once the family had found a holiday home in Cornwall, she had begged every season to stay on beyond the vacation, and when the summer of 1929 turned to autumn, she was finally allowed to remain behind in lodgings with a neighbour in Bodinnick and spend her days writing at Ferryside. As she recalled it in her memoir, *Myself When Young* :

> *It was strange to look across at Ferryside, bolted and shuttered, but I had a key, and went across the first morning, October 3rd, to the desk in my own bedroom, wrapped a rug around my knees, spread sheets of paper and, filling my fountain-pen, wrote in capital letters* THE LOVING SPIRIT.
>
> (Ch. 6, pp.168–169)

At 22, Daphne was determined to gain her independence from her family and immerse herself in writing. London was an exciting place for a young woman, but there were too many distractions, and she longed to pursue her fiction in solitude. The publication of *The Loving Spirit*, completed over a single winter in Cornwall, launched her on a splendid career that was to last for forty years.

Like her two sisters, Angela and Jeanne, Daphne was lucky enough to have had a privileged upbringing that encouraged creative ambitions and allowed her to develop her talents without the need to earn money. The girls had grown up in a big house in Hampstead with all the educational advantages that came with governesses, European travel, and French finishing schools. The success of their father, Gerald, as an actor and theatre manager also exposed them to a scintillating circle of friends and the bohemian influence of the stage. The playwright J.M. Barrie used to call into the nursery to watch the sisters perform his play *Peter Pan*, which had evolved out of his games with Daphne's cousins. The famous actress Gladys Cooper became a sympathetic mother figure to Daphne in London, and Viola Tree was a welcome summer visitor in Cornwall. Of course, no family life is perfect, and being a du Maurier had some distinct disadvantages. Daphne found her mother too distant and her emotionally demanding father too close, especially when she had to face his intense possessiveness about her first dates with young men. But she benefited hugely from her stimulating and liberal environment, and enjoyed all the friendships, parties, and holidays that any attractive young woman could desire.

Daphne, however, had a complex inner life that could be at odds with her outwardly glamorous surroundings. She needed to retreat into the world of her imagination, and she knew from her early teens that she wanted to become a novelist. Books were her constant companions from an early age, as they are for most writers, providing the fuel for her inventive mind. *Myself When Young* records an extraordinary spectrum of influences which can be detected in her adult work, from childhood fairy tales, bible stories, and boys' adventure books like *Treasure Island* and *Mr Midshipman Easy*, to her later diet of Stevenson's *Dr Jekyll and Mr Hyde*, classic stories by Mansfield and Maupassant, the Parisian novels of her grandfather George du Maurier, and the romantic fiction of the Brontës. As an adolescent she started to write seriously, filling notebooks with experimental stories in her commitment to learning her craft.

Cornwall gave her the chance she was searching for to bring her inner and outer lives together in writing *The Loving Spirit*, a story not only composed but set on the River Fowey. Though she would ultimately spend most of her career in Cornwall, she did not initially live there on a permanent basis or see herself as a Cornish novelist. Her next two books, *I'll Never be Young Again* and *The Progress of Julius*, were written in London and ranged ambitiously from Paris to Stockholm and Algiers. Then, after her marriage in 1932 to a handsome and highly decorated army major, Tommy (Boy) Browning, and the arrival of their first child in the following year, her father suddenly died. She channelled her feelings into writing his biography, and produced a lively and disarmingly frank *tour de force*, demonstrating yet again the diversity of her gifts. But despite her proven ability to succeed in such varied genres, Cornwall kept its hold over her imaginative life. It became the setting for the most famous books of her fertile period from 1936 to 1951, when she published *Jamaica Inn*, *Rebecca*, *Frenchman's Creek*, *The King's General* and *My Cousin Rachel* .

DU MAURIER FAMILY TREE

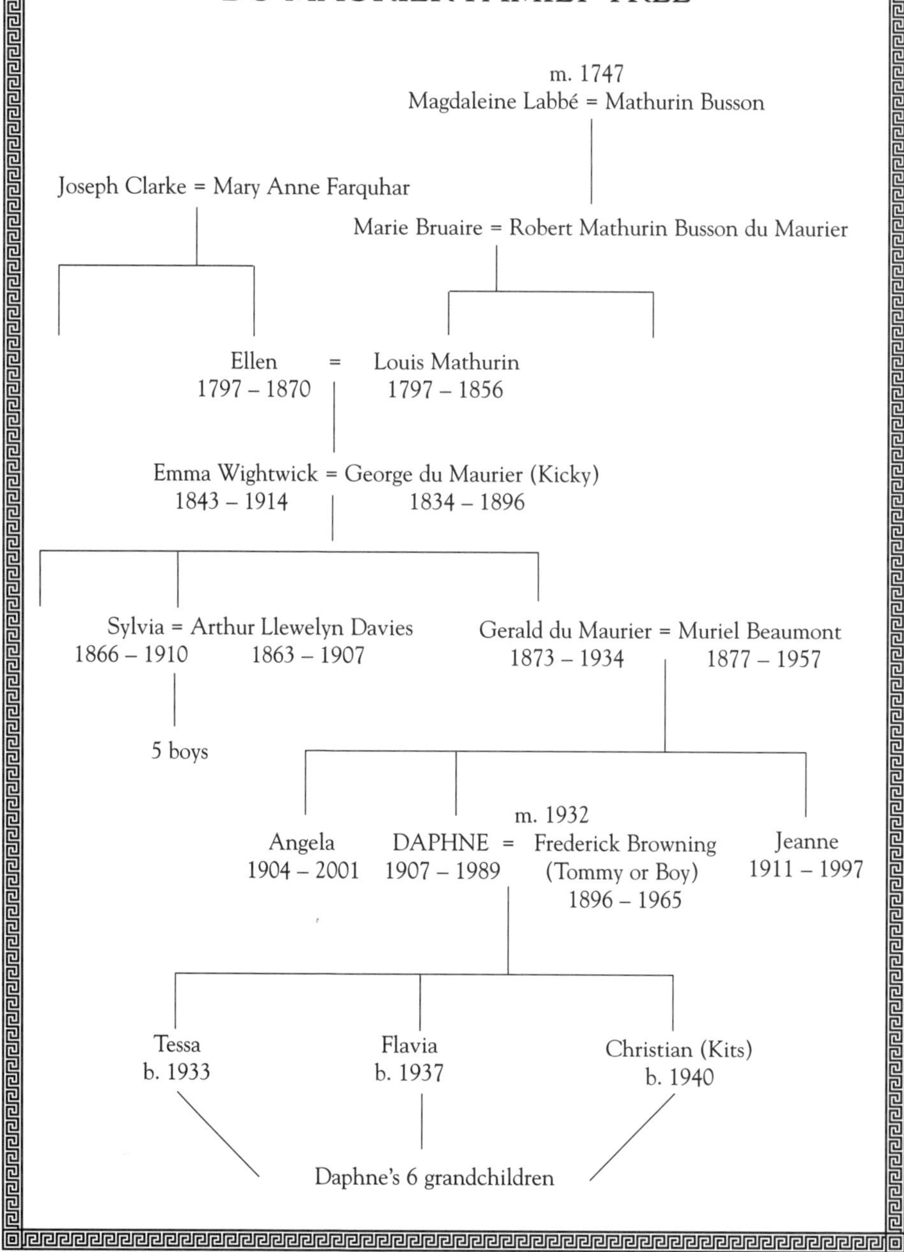

Daphne du Maurier's Houses in Cornwall

FERRYSIDE

A converted boathouse overlooking the River Fowey, acquired by the family in 1926 and still in their possession. Here Daphne wrote her first novel, The Loving Spirit *(1931), a saga based on the history of a local shipbuilding family. Years later, she set a play starring Gertrude Lawrence,* September Tide *(1948), in a similar location called the Ferry House.*

MENABILLY

Daphne's beloved home, leased from the Rashleigh family from 1943 to 1969. This secluded house, set in wooded grounds leading to the sea, was rebuilt in the 19th century. Daphne called Menabilly 'my rat-ridden ruin', but she also admitted: 'I do believe I love Mena more than people.'

Manderley in Rebecca *is in essence Menabilly (the gardens and estate, but not the house). Daphne had trespassed in the overgrown grounds before writing the novel. Aptly, it was the success of the book, and Hitchcock's film, that enabled her to take on the lease.*

The King's General *recreates Menabilly's history during the 17th-century Civil War (before the old house was destroyed by fire).* My Cousin Rachel *and* The Birds *are also set in the coastal area around the Menabilly estate.*

KILMARTH

The Menabilly dower house overlooking the sea, where Daphne lived from 1969 to her death in 1989. The scientific equipment found in the basement provided the germ for The House on the Strand. *The neighbourhood of* Kilmarth *and the nearby village of Par are the locations for Daphne's last novel,* Rule Britannia.

At the same time she was negotiating some crucial life events. She had to contend with acting the role of an army officer's wife, and moving with her husband's job from the quiet of Surrey to the heat of Alexandria. She gave birth to her three children, Tessa, Flavia and Christian (Kits), and once the war began, she found herself having to take care of them with less domestic help. Meanwhile, her distinguished husband was involved in some of the most intense campaigns of the Second World War, becoming the Allied Commander for the operation at Arnhem and then Lord Mountbatten's Chief of Staff in South East Asia. Throughout the war years, his home leaves were rare and brief.

Daphne's Cornish novels over this fifteen-year period were interspersed with very different works: *The du Mauriers*, a family history; *Come Wind, Come Weather*, a collection of uplifting wartime stories for the Moral Re-armament Movement; *Hungry Hill*, an Irish saga; *The Parasites*, a novel about a theatrical family with some similarity to the du Mauriers. She also maintained her connection with the stage by having two plays performed. *The Years Between*, the story of an affair taking place in a country house during the husband's wartime absence, had no link to Cornwall (despite the fact that Daphne's own wartime fling was partly conducted in Fowey), but the second, *September Tide* starring Gertrude Lawrence, was set in a house much like Ferryside.

Margaret Forster's biography makes it clear that Daphne was ambivalent about Tommy's eventual return, fearing that it would impinge on her writing, and rather relieved when he took on the role of managing Princess Elizabeth's household at Clarence House. Daphne was fundamentally loyal to Tommy throughout their lives, though she acknowledged occasional flirtations with other men and on a couple of occasions with women. Interestingly, she claimed that she needed the emotional stimulation of 'menaces', even when they were more fantasy rather than reality, in order to charge her creative thinking. In a letter to the writer Oriel Malet she explained that these people had a function as 'pegs' on whom she could hang a story (*Letters from Menabilly*, p.178). But above all she needed to write, and maintain a domestic routine with her children that protected this precious space, so Tommy's regular absences in London suited her well.

By the end of the war Daphne had moved into Menabilly, the rundown house on the lovely estate near Fowey known to all Daphne's readers as Manderley. With wonderful aptness, it was the pre-war success of *Rebecca* and the profits from Hitchcock's film that gave her the unexpected opportunity to fulfil her longstanding dream of taking a lease from the Rashleigh family. The old house remained her lifelong passion – she once admitted that she loved

The French Connection

In **The Du Mauriers (1937)** *Daphne fictionalises fifty years of her family history, beginning with the unorthodox English childhood of Ellen Clarke, born in 1797. (Ellen's infamous mother, Mary Anne Clarke, the mistress of the Duke of York, became the subject of another novel,* Mary Anne.*) The book follows Ellen and her mother to Paris, where Ellen marries the impecunious scientist Louis Mathurin Busson. In the final part, Ellen's son 'Kicky' moves from France to London and marries there. 'Kicky' is Daphne's grandfather, George du Maurier.*

In the autumn of 1955, Daphne travelled to the Vendôme region of north-west France to find out more about the 18th century du Mauriers, who were master craftsmen in glass. **The Scapegoat (1957)** *shows her new-found respect for the glass-blowers' traditional community values and old-fashioned craftsmanship when the virtuous main character redevelops a French glass foundry as a viable modern business.*

Daphne eventually returned to her topic in **The Glass-Blowers (1963)**, *with the help of researchers in France. The dominant character is Magdaleine, a formidable matriarch, who marries master glass-blower Mathurin Busson in 1747 and takes over the family foundry on her husband's death. The saga, covering a century, unfolds against a carefully depicted provincial background at the time of the French Revolution and its aftermath. Like* The Du Mauriers, *the story ends with George.*

George du Maurier, *Daphne's half-French grandfather, became a pivotal figure in Daphne's sense of her own identity. George moved to London in 1860 and made his name as a cartoonist for* Punch. *He captured his upbringing in France in his illustrated novel* Peter Ibbetson *(1892), and his period as an art student in the Quartier Latin in the bohemian setting of* Trilby *(1894). George's descendants, according to Daphne, are hybrids who 'possess the blood of two countries' and 'hover in their characteristics between England and France.'*

The Family Heirloom

A crystal glass engraved by Mathurin Busson on the occasion of Louis XV's visit to the family foundry, which is passed on to young George at the end of The Glass-Blowers, *stands as an emblem of the unbroken line of the du Mauriers' creative genius. This heirloom was handed down to Daphne and remains in her children's possession.*

'Mena' more than people – and with the help of her housekeeping staff, Daphne wrote on prolifically. Her children grew up there, used to the idiosyncrasies of their rather ramshackle home and their author mother, who tended to be absent-minded when she was 'brewing' one of her novels. Here she found the seclusion that she craved, and her inner and outer lives could run closely together. She lived and wrote at Menabilly for the next 26 years.

In the mid-1960s, after the children had grown up, Daphne's life became more difficult. Following the grief of her husband's death in 1965, she suffered the further wrench of giving up Menabilly to the Rashleigh family. She was depressed, and worried that she might not be able to write creatively again. She moved to Kilmarth, a bright house with wide sea views, only a mile from Menabilly. She had dreaded the loss of her home, but as it turned out, her new location inspired her last novels, *The House on the Strand* and *Rule Britannia.* However, when she died in 1989, she had not brought out a new novel since 1972, and her reputation as well as her sales seemed to be on the decline. She would never know that her books would enjoy a revival so soon after her death.

Daphne's output had continued to be strikingly diverse throughout her career. The final books she wrote at Kilmarth were about the age of Shakespeare, enabling her to boost her flagging imagination with factual material. But however much she wrote with no connection to Cornwall – including excellent Gothic novels like *The Scapegoat* and *The Flight of the Falcon*, and a host of short stories, many of them memorably bizarre – it is as a Cornish writer that she is still remembered.

This guide is designed to encourage the rediscovery of her exciting lesser known writing as well as adding, I hope, to the enjoyment of her wonderful Cornish books.

PART 1

EIGHT BIG THEMES

1 *Daphne's Cornwall*

Cornwall liberated Daphne du Maurier's imagination. At the age of nineteen she fell in love with Fowey, and believed that a new life was opening up before her. I would like to begin with a much-quoted passage from her memoir, which describes that defining moment in Daphne's life – the discovery of the waterside boathouse which was to become Ferryside, the du Mauriers' Cornwall home on the River Fowey – and displays some of the distinctive literary traits which mark her Cornish writing.

Please read extract 1, opposite. What is it, do you think, that makes Daphne's prose so potent?

When you come to these prompts, you may want to make a few notes of your own before reading on.

One of the ways in which Daphne evokes scenes so vividly for the reader is through her arousal of our senses. We detect different smells in the air, and imagine that we can see the rusted chain and river water. The place is described with a passion that literature usually reserves for young love: the meant-to-be-ness of the first meeting ('It could not be mere chance ...'), the vow of total commitment to the other ('I for this, and this for me'), the promise of a rapturously happy future. The writer's imagination bears us onwards, downriver, shifting our gaze from the rope and chain at close range to a longer view. The open sea, invisible from the writer's vantage point on the bank at Ferryside, beckons invitingly from around the headland. The idea of the boundless ocean stirs within the reader a deep desire for escape from the

1. There was a smell in the air of tar and rope and rusted chain, a smell of tidal water. Down harbour, round the point, was the open sea. Here was the freedom I desired, long sought-for, not yet known. Freedom to write, to walk, to wander, freedom to climb hills, to pull a boat, to be alone. It could not be mere chance that brought us to the ferry, and the bottom of Bodinnick hill, and so to the board upon the gate beyond that said For Sale. I remembered a line from a forgotten book, where a lover looks for the first time upon his chosen one – 'I for this, and this for me.'

Daphne du Maurier, *Vanishing Cornwall*, (1967), Prologue, p.6; quoted in her memoir, *Myself When Young*, (1977), pp.102–103 restrictions of everyday life, offering an image of individual freedom that we will encounter many times in Daphne's Cornish fiction.

Daphne set eight of her novels in Cornwall, completing her first book at Ferryside, and spending most of her writing life at Menabilly, but readers are often surprised to learn that she composed some of her best known Cornish books at a great distance. As the young wife of a senior army officer, she found herself writing *Jamaica Inn* in Surrey, *Rebecca* in Alexandria, and *Frenchman's Creek* in wartime Hertfordshire. Yet somehow her yearning for Cornwall made these novels even more atmospheric. They conjure up the extremes of the Cornish landscape, from the wilds of Brontë-esque Bodmin Moor and the craggy north coast of *Jamaica Inn*, to the salty creeks of Cornwall's softer southern shores. The sheltered Helford River becomes the lush green home of the heroine of *Jamaica Inn* and the secret hiding place of the pirate ship in *Frenchman's Creek*.

Rebecca has a memorable topography of its own. Maxim de Winter's house is far grander than Menabilly, but the grounds of Manderley are the same deserted gardens where Daphne had wandered as a trespasser long before taking possession of the property. Explored from the viewpoint of Maxim's shy second wife, Manderley is a threatening place. Its drive in the opening dream sequence is menacingly overgrown, as it was when Daphne first knew it; with blood-red blooms flaunting the exoticism of Cornwall's subtropical gardens. The ironically named Happy Valley leads down to a cove with terrible memories for Maxim; the seas that reach the margins of the estate are changeable and dangerous.

I have chosen a quiet passage from *Rebecca* that contributes to the growing tension of the novel in advance of the dramatic explosions of its major scenes. Here we can see Daphne's experience of the shifting moods of the Cornish coast influencing her fiction.

Please read extract 2, opposite. What use is the writer making of this Cornish seascape?

The gloomy weather and the narrator's depression intensify each other. Though the big seas, surging and roaring, have a romantic grandeur, they are introduced with the unemotive matter-of-factness of a resident who knows only too well how wet and cold a Cornish summer can be. But the background noise of the waves, playing on the narrator's nerves, gradually builds throughout the passage: the murmur is 'low and sullen', 'dull', 'persistent', and

2. *The weather was wet and cold for quite a week, as it often can be in the west country in the early summer, and we did not go down to the beach again. I could see the sea from the terrace, and the lawns. It looked grey and uninviting, great rollers sweeping in to the bay past the beacon on the headland. I pictured them surging into the little cove and breaking with a roar upon the rocks, then running swift and strong to the shelving beach. If I stood on the terrace and listened I could hear the murmur of the sea below me, low and sullen. A dull, persistent sound that never ceased. And the gulls flew inland too, driven by the weather. They hovered above the house in circles, wheeling and crying, flapping their spread wings. I began to understand why some people could not bear the clamour of the sea. It has a mournful harping note sometimes, and the very persistence of it, that eternal roll and thunder and hiss, plays a jagged tune upon the nerves. I was glad our rooms were in the east wing and I could lean out of my window and look down upon the rose-garden.*

Daphne du Maurier *Rebecca* (1938), ch.11, p.134

Daphne's Cornish Writing

Novels	
1931	*THE LOVING SPIRIT*
1936	*JAMAICA INN*
1938	*REBECCA*
1941	*FRENCHMAN'S CREEK*
1946	*THE KING'S GENERAL*
1951	*MY COUSIN RACHEL*
1962	*CASTLE DOR (with Sir Arthur Quiller-Couch)*
1969	*THE HOUSE ON THE STRAND*
1972	*RULE BRITANNIA*
Stories	
1952	*THE BIRDS*
Play	
1949	*SEPTEMBER TIDE*
Non-fiction	
1967	*VANISHING CORNWALL*

'mournful'. The crying of the gulls over Manderley adds a haunting note to the breakers' 'eternal roll and thunder and hiss.' There is no escape from the presence of the sea, which will soon play its vital part in uncovering the novel's mystery. The waters are Rebecca's element – she loved her boat and her beach-side boathouse – and the cove which Maxim's second wife visualises in this extract is where her yacht went down. The narrator already knows that her husband hates the place, and the sound of the breakers is a perpetual warning that something in her marriage is terribly wrong. The domestic storm, the reader senses, will eventually break. When a steamer runs aground in the fog and the waves give up their secrets, the truth of Rebecca's death will begin to emerge, and Maxim's desperate efforts to suppress the guilty knowledge submerged in the depths of his psyche will be similarly doomed to failure. We can already feel that there is no hope for his wife's timid attempts to enjoy the east wing and the quiet of the rose-garden; she can no more succeed in shutting out the 'roar upon the rocks', clearly audible from Rebecca's bedroom on the other side of the house, than she can avoid the legacy of Rebecca at Manderley.

Cornwall may be a place of natural beauty and rural retreat, but its dangerous coastlines – as *Rebecca* forcefully illustrates – can be appropriated to brilliant effect in representing the extreme emotions of unbridled desire or unbearable despair.

For many people who love to wander in the most remote and lightly inhabited parts of the region, like Daphne du Maurier, Cornwall seems to have a further dimension in the rich history that hovers so close to the surface of its unbuilt landscapes. Stealing back into the past on the Helford River is the theme of *Frenchman's Creek*'s opening chapter, where the reader's ears catch 'the echoes of that other time' when a pirate 'whistled softly from the dark belt of trees', and the leisure sailor, exploring in his dinghy on a midsummer night, is suddenly aware of 'the deep silence of the creek', and feels uneasily that he is 'an interloper, a trespasser in time' (pp.3–4). For anyone who has fished Cornwall's dark rivers at night, mused in the grounds of gracious manor houses, walked the grass-covered fort of Castle Dor, explored the traces of ancient Iron Age dwellings, lost her way among the bogs of Bodmin Moor, or dared to enter the graveyard of the Reverend Hawker's church at dusk, where the pale figurehead of the wrecked *Caledonia* glimmers above the buried remains of drowned sailors, it takes a very small leap of the imagination indeed to believe that you might encounter a ghost or two from another century, or glide back into an earlier age. In Daphne's late novel *The House on the Strand*, which was written during her move to Kilmarth, a house believed to be built on medieval foundations, she takes her boldest time trip of all. The narrator of the novel uses a drug to enter the fourteenth-century world of his predecessor, one Roger Kylmerth, slipping into the past with a frightening ease that makes disaster inevitable.

The King's General is a novel set entirely in the past, in the troubled period of the Civil War. There is no transition from the present to the seventeenth century: the book begins with the words of Honor Harris, dated September 1653. For readers who know their Civil War history, the fighting is at an end, and the country will shortly fall under the rule of Oliver Cromwell as Lord Protector; Honor's life is coming towards its end too, and the appendix to the book, 'What Happened to the People in the Story', confirms that the historical character on whom she is based died only two months later, in November 1653. Of course we will not find out this fact until we finish the novel, and we don't need to know it; the tone of the opening page is elegiac enough to convey the sense of Honor's life ebbing naturally away.

Please read extract 3, opposite, from *The King's General*. Why do we sense that the speaker is ageing?

The season is on the turn, from late summer to autumn. The air becomes colder, and day seems to move more slowly; the sun is 'laggard' (the only archaic word in these lines to indicate that the speaker's language is different from our own) and droplets hang undried and unshaken on the grasses. The approach of winter hints at the idea of death as inevitable and acceptable. Honor measures her day by the ebb and flow of the tides, and it is the falling waters that draw her seaward – described in a single, long, graceful, sweeping sentence. There is an old superstition which tells of dying people waiting for the turn of the tide to release their souls. The impression, lightly made on the reader's mind, is of someone calmly awaiting the end.

Daphne is here at the height of her powers, luring us into the mysterious web of someone else's mind. (This is, after all, the author who casts her spell over the reader of *Rebecca* with those bewitching words: 'Last night I dreamt I went to Manderley again.') The delicate imagery of Honor's first

3. *September, 1653. The last of summer. The first chill winds of autumn. The sun no longer strikes my eastern window as I wake, but, turning laggard, does not top the hill before eight o'clock. A white mist hides the bay sometimes until noon, and hangs about the marshes too, leaving, when it lifts, a breath of cold air behind it. Because of this, the tall grass in the meadow never dries, but long past midday shimmers and glistens in the sun, the great drops of moisture hanging motionless upon the stems. I notice the tides more than I did once. They seem to make a pattern to the day. When the water drains from the marshes, and little by little the yellow sands appear, rippling and hard and firm, it seems to my foolish fancy, as I lie here, that I too go seaward with the tide, and all my old hidden dreams that I thought buried for all time are bare and naked to the day, just as the shells and the stones are on the sands.*

Daphne du Maurier *The King's General* (1946), ch.1, p.1

paragraph sensitises the reader, imperceptibly drawing us into her thoughts when she is at her most vulnerable. As the falling tide leaves her buried dreams exposed on the rippling sands, a picture forms of her psyche, the waters receding to reveal hidden guilts and desires. The reader prepares to make the journey with Honor while she lapses back into her personal past. *The King's General* will have its fill of dramatic action – falcon hunting, battles, rivalries, love affairs and a secret passage – but it will be Honor's shrewd observations, her mature reflections and her deepest feelings, that guide us through the story.

Considering these three passages together, we realise that Daphne du Maurier is not writing about one Cornwall, even when she returns to the same place. The coastal settings in the

extracts we have been looking at are only a few miles apart in reality, but they appear utterly different because they are seen through the minds of different narrators. Daphne writes always out of her transforming imagination, and therefore gives us as many Cornwalls as there are chapters in her Cornish books.

2 Early heroines

If you cross on the ferry from the Fowey side of the river to Bodinnick, you can see the freshly restored figurehead of the Jane Slade, buxom and resplendent, under the window of the upstairs room at Ferryside where Daphne wrote her first novel, *The Loving Spirit*. Her saga followed the fortunes of a local shipbuilding family through four generations, beginning with the remarkable Jane Slade. At the end of the first (and best) part of the book – which Daphne claimed to have finished in a fortnight – the spirit of her dying heroine, renamed Janet Coombe, enters the ship named after her. Released from her woman's body she is free to leap and plunge, like her figurehead, through the high seas.

Daphne was revelling in her new-found independence, and *The Loving Spirit* is imbued with her personal optimism that she would be able to fulfil her identity in Cornwall, and exercise all the unfeminine freedoms she invoked in her diary – 'to write, to walk, ... to pull a boat, to be alone.' As a teenager, she had cut her creative teeth on cynical stories that put women in a seedy light in their relationships with even nastier men, but *The Loving Spirit* is a new departure. There is a lot of the author in Janet Coombe, and – as with Dona St Columb in *Frenchman's Creek* – readers are tempted into identifying with her. You might suspect that Daphne is simply relapsing into the stereotypes of popular fiction, but Janet and Dona do not match the hoydenish heroines of conventional romantic novels, who are ultimately tamed by mating with the man of their dreams. In du Maurier's books, marriage does not close off the pursuit of unsatisfied desires. This section looks more closely at the unresolvable dilemma facing two of her most attractive heroines.

From the opening pages of *The Loving Spirit*, the reader is caught up in the contradictory forces vying within Jane Coombe. We meet her alone among the birds and gorse bushes on the hill above the harbour of Plyn, where she feels a sense of escape likened to 'the shy fluttering wings of a bird.' This is the morning of her wedding day. Though she is ready for marriage to her boat-builder cousin, Thomas, she is conscious that 'there were two sides of her; one that wanted to be the wife of a man, and to care for him and love him tenderly, and one that asked only to be part of a ship, part of the seas and the sky above, with the glad free ways of a gull' (p.9). As a child she had prayed to grow up into a lad, and as a woman she can never entirely abandon her carefree tomboy ways.

Once married, Janet plays the part of a contented wife, but at times she yearns for more, something 'strong and primitive' (p.11) that will go beyond the marital bond. One Christmas Eve, she stays at home with her small children rather than accompanying her husband to midnight mass.

Please read extract 4, opposite. What influences are at work on Janet?

The homely details of sleeping children and hot broth add to the picture of Janet's domestic life which has been built up over the previous pages. The pull of her family is obviously very strong. But the cosy cottage seems too small for her, as she leans out of the window and hears the sea. The moon, one of nature's most powerful forces, associated with the female cycle, is high in the sky, and the 'call' she feels is deeply intuitive: 'she knew that she must go to the cliffs.' Once there she is in harmony with the elements, 'possessed with the strange power and clarity of the moon itself', and enters another dimension, overcome by a supernatural vision. What we don't yet know is that the man she sees, whose need is so compelling that it can draw her into the future to comfort him, represents the closest instinctive bond of all – and until you have read on in this novel for yourself, it is not fair to explain. You may think at the end of this extract that the figure of the man is a lover, so cleverly does du Maurier play with the formulae of romantic fiction, but it is not long before the reader finds out otherwise. Even in her first novel, Daphne's writing is never straightforward or predictable.

In its blending of two fictional modes, romance and realism, *The Loving Spirit* is recognisably in the Brontë tradition. Charlotte Brontë's *Jane Eyre*, for example, describes Jane's everyday life and surroundings as if she were a real woman in a normal social situation, yet allows Rochester to reach her with his telepathic cry when he is in greatest need of her. Emily Brontë's *Wuthering Heights* is even bolder in its mixing of the mundane and the supernatural, and

4. Janet was now alone in the house with the two children, who were sleeping soundly in the room above. She prepared some hot broth for her husband when he should return from the church, cold and hungry from his prayers and his walk.

She wrapped her shawl about her shoulders and leant from the window. A faint film of snow still lay upon the ground.

The moon was high in the sky, and there was no sound but the moan of the still water lapping the rocks beyond the harbour. Suddenly she knew that she must go to the cliffs, and follow the call of her heart.

She hid the key of the door in her bodice and left the house. It seemed to her that there were wings to her body that bore her swiftly away from home and the sleeping children, away up the steep, narrow street of Plyn, to the white-frosted hills and the silent sky.

She leant against the Castle ruins with the sea at her feet, and the light of the moon on her face. Then she closed her eyes, and the jumbled thoughts fled from her mind, her tired body seemed to slip away from her, and she was possessed with the strange power and clarity of the moon itself. When she opened her eyes for a moment there was a mist about her, and when it dissolved she saw kneeling beside the cliff with his head bowed in his hands, the figure of a man.

Daphne du Maurier *The Loving Spirit* (1931), ch.5, p.32

it is Emily who is Daphne's acknowledged inspiration for her novel. Each part of the book begins with a quotation from her impassioned poetry, and the phrase 'loving spirit' is taken from her work. Emily's stature gives Daphne the licence she requires to take elements from romance writing without feeling that she is lowering her standards to the level of popular women's fiction. *The Loving Spirit* has all the circumstantial detail of a historical novel, but is not afraid to call on intuition and reach for the infinite.

Intriguingly, Daphne could have given very different answers to Janet Coombe's dilemma if she had written a realist novel that followed more closely the actual biography of her nineteenth-century prototype, Jane Slade. For the role of helpmeet and partner to a skilled craftsman, who was running his own boatbuilding business in the heart of an economically flourishing community, could have provided Janet with a fulfilling life within the confines of Plyn. The original Jane Slade outlived her husband, and research by the maritime historian Helen Doe has shown that she continued to run the local inn while taking over responsibility for the successful management of the Slade boatyard. But Daphne's decision to polarise the cottage and the cliffs, ignoring the option of empowering Janet Coombe within her family and community, indicates that she was more interested in women with an unconventional spirit than in practical feminist achievement.

On bringing her saga up to date, Daphne was once again faced with a decision. The heroine of the book's final segment, Janet's great-granddaughter Jennifer Coombe, is Daphne's contemporary, brought up in London but drawn back to her birthplace. In the last pages, we learn that she is married to the cousin who inherited the family boatyard, now building racing yachts for a lucrative leisure market, and we might expect a modern educated woman to be playing a different role from her great-grandmother. But Jennifer's involvement in the business seems minimal, as she happily occupies the woman's traditional place of homemaker without suffering from the inner conflict faced by the indomitable Janet. It makes a thought-provoking postscript to the novel to learn that Daphne was shortly to be confronted with the same choices as Janet and Jennifer Coombe. *The Loving Spirit* was finished in January 1930 and published in the following year. One of its readers, no doubt attracted to the book by the publicity that had been generated by the author's du Maurier name, was Tommy Browning, a dashing army major, who invited Daphne out on a sailing date in April 1932. Three months later, they were married in the church at Lanteglos above Polruan (the parish church where Janet Coombe's husband attended the midnight service on Christmas Eve), and Daphne soon

Jane Slade (1813–1885)

The family saga of The Loving Spirit *is based on the Slade family of Polruan. The life of Jane Slade, the inspiration for Daphne's fictional matriarch, Janet Coombe, has been vividly documented in Helen Doe's illustrated book* Jane Slade of Polruan *(Truran 2002). These highlights show what an extraordinary woman Jane was.*

1813 *Jane Symons Salt, daughter of a local sea captain, was born in Polruan on the Fowey estuary.*
1831 *Jane married Christopher Slade on completion of his seven-year apprenticeship as a shipwright. Jane's father opened the Russell Inn, which was managed by the young couple. Christopher worked as an independent shipwright and invested, as did many local people, in the building of local ships and trading ventures. They had nine surviving children.*
1847 *As the economic slump of the 1840s drew to an end, Jane's father and husband took out a mortgage on the Russell Inn and set up a shipyard.*
1870 *The schooner, the* Jane Slade *– the first ship to be built in their own yard that Jane and Christopher planned to own themselves – was nearing completion when Christopher (not Jane, as in Daphne's novel) died suddenly of heart disease.*

The Jane Slade *was launched later in 1870 from the Slades' yard at Polruan, bearing the fine figurehead of Jane herself, which now can be seen a little further up the River Fowey on the du Mauriers' house, Ferryside. The ship was captained by Jane's second son, Thomas, now a qualified master mariner; his youngest brother Albert joined him as an ordinary seaman on the* Jane Slade's *maiden voyage. Jane took over her late husband's role as head of the shipbuilding business, which now bore her name: Mrs Jane Slade & Sons.*

Her eldest son William, working with two of his brothers, managed the shipbuilding. Jane ran the business side, as well as the Russell Inn. She was the majority shareholder in the Jane Slade, *and an investor in a large number of other ships. Even when she retired at the age of 67, she retained the role of ship's accountant. By then her grandson was already halfway through his seven-year apprenticeship at the yard.*
1885 *Jane died at the age of 72.*

found herself a married woman with children on the way. Her personal experience of family life seems to have made her even more aware of the divergent demands on women, which could mean that settling down was the most difficult option of all.

Daphne conceived Dona St Columb in very different circumstances from her creation of Janet Coombe – during a long wartime separation from her husband when the attractions of an easily available affair proved all too irresistible. *Frenchman's Creek*, luckily for readers looking for romance, reflects all the fun of such a dalliance and little of the angst. We will meet Dona the romantic heroine again, in the next section, but now it is time to reflect on the more serious divisions in her identity – a rather more glamorous variant on Janet's cottage-or-cliffs dilemma – as she is pulled between her Helford mansion and her pirate masquerades.

Dona plays a breeches part that any would-be tomboy must envy. Before the story begins with her escape to her Cornish estate, she has been drinking alongside actresses and whores with her husband's fashionable men-friends in London taverns, and though she has foresworn her frivolous town life as being somehow unworthy of her true self, there are later memorable incidents of highly unfeminine audacity. Whether she is wagering her ruby ear-rings for a lock from Lord Godolphin's wig, or sailing out of Fowey Harbour on the stolen *Merry Fortune*, dressed as a boy, with cannon balls falling around the ship, the exhilarated reader cannot help but enjoy her adventures. Nevertheless, they hardly disclose a personality of any depth, and the distance between the old city Dona and the new country Dona is so far barely in evidence.

But there are quiet moments of reflection in *Frenchman's Creek*, which withdraw from the swashbuckling action to allow the reader to glimpse something more of Dona's inner life.

Please read extract 5, opposite. What do we find out about Dona's identity and choices?

5. *So* La Mouette *stole in once more towards the land ... The cable rattled with a hollow sound in the deep pool beneath the trees, and the ship swung round to meet the last of the flood tide, and suddenly from nowhere came a swan and his mate, like two white barges sailing in company, and following them three cygnets, soft and brown. They went away down the creek, leaving a wake behind them as a vessel would ...*

The captain's boat waited beneath the ladder ... and they pulled away down the creek where the swans had gone, the little boat lapping against the water. Soon the fire glowed in the clearing, the dried sticks snapping and breaking ...

'And this,' she said, watching the fire, 'could be forever, if we wished ...'

'You forget,' he said, 'that women are more primitive than men. For a time they will wander, yes, and play at love, and play at adventure. And then, like the birds, they must make their nest. Instinct is too strong for them. Birds build the home they crave, and settle down into it, warm and safe, and have their babies ... So you see, my Dona, there is no escape for a woman, only for a night and for a day.'

'No, you are right,' she said, 'there is no escape for a woman. Therefore if I sail with you again I shall be a cabin-boy, and borrow Pierre Blanc's breeches ...'

Daphne du Maurier *Frenchman's Creek* (1941), ch.15, pp.145–148

In this extract, the pirate ship *La Mouette* – named after the sea-going gull which symbolises desire for freedom – is returning to the secrecy of *Frenchman's Creek* after a successful raid on Fowey. Dona's daring escapade with her French pirate lover, indeed her entire Cornish journey, have represented an expression of unfulfilled desires which she herself barely understands. She is pressing at the envelope of her own identity, crossing the boundaries of her old self, yet finding that her affectionate children, if not her unrefined husband, are drawing her back to her home life, even while she savours the excitement of her reckless liberty.

The imagery of the evening scene reinforces the natural pull of the family, as the swan and his mate, more sedate than the freewheeling gull, lead their cygnets down the creek. But significantly it is the Frenchman, not Dona, who is arguing here for a biological imperative that embeds instinctive home-making in the female psyche – and in Chapter 7 it is another man, her steward William, who puts a similar case. Dona, for her part, resists the closure of the conversation. Even as she admits to a woman's unbreakable ties to her children, she insists on proposing fancifully to become *La Mouette's* cabin-boy, a boy-woman who can evade her adult responsibilities, and the full sexual relationship that in the natural course of things turns lovers into parents – and goes off to play, like Peter Pan, with the pirates.

Her dialogues with the Frenchman often preserve this ambiguity, this sense of a conundrum unresolved. The differences between men and women, lovers and friends, childhood and adulthood, the settling-down self and the unsatisfied, desiring self, are never finally resolved in any du Maurier novel. Here, the sounds in the creek – the loud hollow rattle of the cable as the ship anchors, the quieter lap of the rowing boat, the 'snapping and breaking' of the sticks on the fire – strain the ears and increase the reader's tense expectancy. The effect is not only to intensify the erotic charge of the lovers' meeting, but also to make us listen more intently to their conversation. We wonder whether we will catch a few meaningful words in their intimate exchanges that will reveal to us, and to Dona herself, what it is that a woman really wants. Is it motherhood or male freedom? The cottage or the cliffs? The mansion or the masquerade? These are questions which Daphne, like most women, never felt able to answer.

3 *Romance with a big R*

Writing *Frenchman's Creek* during the war, Daphne promised her publisher Victor Gollancz that she would produce 'a romance with a big R!', the kind of escapist fantasy calculated to take readers' minds away from the daily round of wartime privations. And she certainly succeeded in writing a big romance in two senses. As well as being an adventure story of pirate raids and derring do, in direct line of descent from Daphne's childhood favourite *Treasure Island*, *Frenchman's Creek* is quintessentially a love story.

When I once asked a group of Daphne du Maurier fans (in which longstanding married couples happened to predominate) to reflect for a moment on the idea of romantic love, they came up with the wonderfully paradoxical definition, 'perpetual ecstasy'. Romantic love is seen as a concept impossible to fulfil in practice, since ecstasy describes an emotional peak that cannot be prolonged, let alone sustained perpetually through life's ups and downs. Even the most ardent devotees of romantic fiction had to accede to the group's gently cynical amusement at the very thought of a Romeo and Juliet relationship that could last for ever. Daphne would certainly have agreed. The no-nonsense opening of one of her essays firmly asserts:

> *There is no such thing as romantic love. This is a statement of fact, and I defy all those who hold a contrary opinion. Romantic love is an illusion ...*
> *('Romantic Love', in Daphne du Maurier* The Rebecca Notebook and Other Memories, *p.99)*

The most intensely romantic legends – Romeo and Juliet, Tristan and Isolda – find a way out of the bind. Such myths end not with a wedded future, but with the lovers' tragically early parting and death, which preserve the brief period of ecstasy undiminished. Some romantic novels follow suit. Rosamunde Pilcher's *The Shell Seekers*, a Cornish novel loved by many of Daphne du Maurier's admirers, kills off the hero in the war, decades before the end of the book. Such lovers can be reunited in death, their passion youthful and unspoilt by the messiness of marriage. Other novels follow the alternative formula of gesturing optimistically down the Pemberley path in the last chapter; but this is an option in which Daphne du Maurier never indulges.

Frenchman's Creek follows the Tristan and Isolda route, though in the vein of comedy rather than tragedy. It traces the meeting and inevitable parting of adulterous lovers, who are free beyond death to haunt the quiet waters of the Helford in blissful union for ever. The adventures of the gentlewoman Dona St Columb, with her distinguished Frenchman and his pirate crew, are among the most carefree pages in all of Daphne's fiction. If you like to think of her as a romantic writer, savour them now as deeply as you can, for we will soon be getting to know a very different Daphne!

What is your idea of romantic love? Does the affair between Dona and her pirate in extract 6 fulfil your definition?

You will surely have found this passage unashamedly romantic. The sensuality of the lovers' salty lips and wet hair, the excitement of the spray and the 'high-crested sea' in the opening lines are enhanced by the breathlessness of the first sentence, in which the phrases rise and fall without a stop, wave-like, until they rest on the vivid words: 'and his hair was wet.' The vignette of the Frenchman drawing a heron gives a glimpse of an ideal man, not only a bold rover, but a sensitive artist responding to the delicate beauty of a bird; the image of his ship 'stealing in towards the land' is a potent evocation of their clandestine meetings. True lovers' belief in their destiny is here too. The encounter is something that 'nothing could prevent'; Dona is 'part of his body and part of his mind.' They are, in accordance with the creed of romantic love, two halves of a perfect whole, incomplete without each other.

Yet there is already a hint here that their happiness is imperfect, or at least untenable. Instead of the passage ending with the statement that 'they belonged to each other,' summing up all that has gone before, there is a further coda to the sentence that, for me, is utterly typical of Daphne's writing. When she adds that they are 'both wanderers, both fugitives, cast in the same mould,' I catch a slightly plaintive note, as haunting as a curlew's cry along the river. Wanderers and fugitives are fleeing a settled life; it is not in their nature to seek

6. Once again the spray rose from the top of a high-crested sea, as the ship crossed the bar at the mouth of the estuary, and Dona, smiling, tasted it on her lips, and looking up, saw that the Frenchman had left the helmsman and was standing beside her, and the spray must have caught him too, for there was salt upon his lips and his hair was wet.

'Do you like it?' he said, and she nodded, laughing up at him, so that he smiled an instant, looking towards the sea. As he did so she was filled with a great triumph and a sudden ecstasy, for she knew then that he was hers, and she loved him, and that it was something she had known from the very beginning, from the first moment when she had walked into his cabin and found him sitting at the table drawing the heron. Or before that even, when she had seen the ship on the horizon stealing in towards the land, she had known then that this thing was to happen, that nothing could prevent it; she was part of his body and part of his mind, they belonged to each other, both wanderers, both fugitives, cast in the same mould.

Daphne du Maurier *Frenchman's Creek* (1941), ch.10, p.102

Cornish Romance

Jamaica Inn and Frenchman's Creek are in the mainstream Treasure Island tradition of adventure novels, featuring smugglers, wreckers and pirates. But they also have their place in a sub-genre of romantic fiction with distinctively Cornish settings. Here are some 19th-century examples.

Dead Man's Rock *(1887) by Sir Arthur Quiller-Couch, Daphne's distinguished literary friend in Fowey, launched Q's career in fiction. A historical romance of wrecked ships and buried treasure set on the south coast of Cornwall.*

The Watchers on the Longships *(1876) by James F. Cobb builds a strong Methodist message into a thrilling adventure story. The clergyman hero has a mission to build a lighthouse to warn ships away from the dangerous Longships islands off Land's End, but local people bitterly resent his plan to deny them their pickings from the wrecks. Secondhand copies of this novel are easy to find, but many are falling apart from overuse — evidence that this moralising Sunday School prize book was also a loved bestseller.*

The Christian plot of The Watchers *runs contrary to the usual depiction of parsons in Cornish legend. When Robert Stephen Hawker became vicar of Morwenstow in 1834, he found that the clergy were expected to collude in local customs, and tells the story of one minister who held the lantern while his parishioners went about the business of stripping a wreck. In such stories we can see hints of Daphne's wicked vicar of Altarnun in* Jamaica Inn.

In the Roar of the Sea *(1892) by the prolific Devon romance writer Sabine Baring-Gould takes its diabolical villain, Cruel Coppinger, from a legend revived (and no doubt largely invented) by Parson Hawker. Baring-Gould's Coppinger is not only a smuggler, bringing goods into Cornwall in his ship, the* Black Prince, *but a callous wrecker, who lures ships onto Doom Bar with false lights. (A moving light, tied on the head of a donkey as it walks the uneven cliff paths, allegedly gives the impression of another ship on the sea.) The novel's bold heroine, Judith Trevisa, who bravely stands up to ruthless wreckers on the dangerous Cornish coast, is a worthy predecessor of du Maurier's indomitable Mary Yellan in* Jamaica Inn.

Smuggling was rife in Cornwall, especially in the 18th century; privateers, French and otherwise, raided the coast; and no doubt, in some poor villages, the wreck of a ship with valuable cargo was welcomed as a providential event. But there is no evidence of deliberate wrecking. However, historical truth plays little part in the lurid picture of Celtic lawlessness painted in Victorian fiction. This image of Cornwall as a wild barbarous periphery was perpetuated throughout the 20th century by countless popular novelists (and the tourist industry) – and brilliantly exploited by Daphne du Maurier.

contentment. In the last section we examined Dona's dilemma more closely, since she was a married woman who could not spend the rest of her life roaming the seas with the pirates without abandoning her children. But these lovers' joy is surely fleeting, children or not, since its quality depends on hidden creeks, risky raids, and snatched meetings. The transient intensity of their relationship is the very condition that enables Daphne to capture the ardour of their affair; the reader will not easily forget the adrenalin rush of their reckless exploits. In the story of Dona and her Frenchman, Daphne du Maurier fulfils her readers' highest expectations by celebrating that impossible, heady illusion of romantic love.

For many holiday readers of du Maurier's fiction, who select the half-remembered title *Frenchman's Creek* from the bookshops of Fowey or Jamaica Inn, Dona may be the only heroine they know. Daphne would have been mortified. Far from revelling in a fantasy world of gallant pirates and devoted ladies, she was repeatedly drawn to the suffering of lonely people and the display of less admirable passions. Though a special plea can be made for the mid-life lovers in *The King's General*, which we shall consider later in the book, it is generally true to say that most of Daphne's work is dominated by her darker side. So in order to begin to understand the themes that obsessed her in so much of her writing, I will contrast the flamboyant *Frenchman's Creek* with her more typically bitter anti-romance, *My Cousin Rachel.*

When Philip Ashley falls desperately in love with Rachel, his uncle's Italian widow, he is a naive young man, quickly out of his emotional depth. Daphne was intrigued by men's inadequacies, especially their helplessness in the throes of desire for women, returning to this theme throughout her career from her second book, *I'll Never Be Young* Again, to her penultimate novel, *The House on the Strand.* (They are both discussed in later sections, along with *The*

Scapegoat, *The Flight of the Falcon*, 'Not After Midnight' and 'Monte Verità', all of which have male narrators.) Typically the men long for another, richer life, often personified in an unattainable woman. Scholarly English John in *The Scapegoat* enjoys the warm attentions of a mature mistress only for a week, when he take on the guise of a Frenchman, and middle-aged Dick in *The House on the Strand* yearns hopelessly after a beautiful lady who once slept in his house six centuries before his time. Daphne's anti-heroes long for their love to be reciprocated, and are rarely satisfied.

Philip is besotted with Cousin Rachel, an older woman, a foreigner, and the wife who may have subjected his dear uncle Ambrose to mental torment in the closing months of his life in Italy. Alone with him on his Cornish estate, Rachel can seem to Philip to be a gentle, feminine and understanding woman, but he realises with bitterness that she places little value on their occasional nights of lovemaking, and her real feelings are impenetrable. When her lawyer Rainaldi pays her a visit, she reverts to being an incomprehensible and alien presence within the familiar walls of his rural home.

How is Rachel's Italian origin used in extract 7a, opposite, to reinforce Philip's suspicions of her character?

Dark in appearance and dark in nature, Italians have played a sinister part in English culture from legends of the medieval Borgias, through a century of Gothic fiction, to Henry James's late Victorian tales of innocent New World heroines imprisoned in an ancient Italian culture tainted by the cruelties of a pagan past. Whereas Dona's pirate is enhanced by his foreignness, the reputation of elegant and seductive Frenchmen making the English gentry look stolid by comparison, an Italian lawyer with 'dark hooded eyes' can be read only as sinister and snake-like. Philip's jealousy of Rainaldi for his intimacy with Rachel means that the reader cannot trust his spiteful judgement, but we have no other evidence to go on. The solid values associated with the Ashley house and land, with the family retainer and the old panelled dining-room that Philip has inherited, encourage us to conspire with him in imagining a very different, somehow dishonest, Italian dinner, with 'smooth dark servants' and meretricious 'glitter'. Rachel is tainted by her Italian speech, a strange language spoken with unmeasured swiftness, and by her hard 'brilliance'. Simply by being foreign, she becomes the classic femme fatale, mysterious and irresistible, manipulative and possibly deadly. Philip's inability to comprehend the nature of his cousin Rachel casts a dark shadow over the plot. Was she an

7a. ... now and again Rachel would put out her hand to me across the table, as she would do to a child, and say, 'You must forgive us, Philip dear. It is so long since I have seen Rainaldi,' while he watched me with those dark hooded eyes, and slowly smiled.

Once or twice they broke into Italian. ... She would answer him, and as she spoke and I heard the unfamiliar words pour from her lips, so much faster surely than when we talked together in English, it was as though her whole cast of countenance was changed; she became more animated and more vivid, yet harder in a sense, and with a new brilliance that I did not like so well.

It seemed to me that the pair of them were ill-placed at my table, in the panelled dining-room; they should have been elsewhere, in Florence or in Rome, with smooth dark servants waiting on them and all the glitter of a society foreign to me ...

Daphne du Maurier *My Cousin Rachel* (1951), Ch.20, p.226

7b. They used to hang men at Four Turnings in the old days.

Not any more, though. Now, when a murderer pays the penalty for his crime, he does so up at Bodmin, after fair trial at the Assizes. That is, if the law convicts him, before his own conscience kills him. It is better so. Like a surgical operation. And the body has decent burial, though a nameless grave. When I was a child it was otherwise. I can remember as a little lad seeing a fellow hang in chains where the four roads meet. His face and body were blackened with tar for preservation. He hung there for five weeks before they cut him down, and it was the fourth week that I saw him.

Daphne du Maurier *My Cousin Rachel* (1951), Ch.1, p.1

unscrupulous poisoner, or a mere opportunist? At the end, he can never be sure, and all he is left with is his guilt.

We know from the start of the story that the narrator will never escape the living hell of his uncertainty. Philip's guilt is disgustingly embodied in the corpse of a criminal rotting in chains at Four Turnings, on the edge of his estate, a public punishment for a local man who killed his wife. The book's opening lines:

> *They used to hang men at Four Turnings in the old days.*
> *Not any more, though.*

are echoed at its close, confirming that Philip has to endure an endless cycle of torment about a past that can never be put right.

My Cousin Rachel is a typical du Maurier love story, embroiled in frustration, misery, even murder. Daphne was right to insist that *Frenchman's Creek* was a one off – her only real 'romance with a big R.'

Before leaving this section, have a look at extract 7b, the beginning of *My Cousin Rachel*. Be honest! Can you ever think of Daphne du Maurier as a romantic writer again?

4 *House of secrets*

In an essay called 'The House of Secrets', written after her wartime move to Menabilly, Daphne describes the progress of her fifteen-year love affair with the house before she unexpectedly gained possession. On the first occasion in 1928, when she trespassed in the overgrown grounds with her sister Angela, they were overtaken by dusk and abandoned their search for the hidden house. According to Angela's evocative account, in her memoir *It's Only The Sister*, this autumnal outing was an 'eerie and most ghost-like' experience:

> *Owls by now were hooting, and strange night birds emitted shrieks and cries, the unmistakable smell of fox was frequently apparent and the dogs kept at our heels, tails down, all enjoyment vanished. We knew that many people said Menabilly was haunted, and by now I was convinced that local superstition had not lied.* (Ch.6, p.140)

But here the sisters' versions diverge, for Angela claims that they set off the next day and were successful in locating the house together. When they did reach it, and gazed through the dirty windows at Victorian furniture and an old rocking-horse, she found it a frightening and gloomy place. Intriguingly, whether consciously or not, Daphne has obliterated that occasion from her essay (though she reinstated it later in *Myself When Young*). In this account, she finds Menabilly for the first time in the following spring, when she is alone. Having left at dawn to row across the river from Ferryside, she makes her way on foot into the estate from Polridmouth Bay, past the cottage that she would later transform into Rebecca's boathouse.

Think about the mood of the scene described in extract 8a overleaf. How does the picture of Menabilly compare with the lines about Manderley in extract 8b?

8a. I paused, stung by the beauty of that first pink glow of sunrise on the water, but the path led on, and I would not be deterred … I was hard upon it now, the place I sought. Some instinct made me crouch upon my belly and crawl softly to the wet grass at the foot of the shrubs. The morning mist was lifting, and the sun was coming up above the trees even as the moon had done last autumn. This time there was no owl, but blackbird, thrush and robin greeting the summer day.

I edged my way on to the lawn, and there she stood. My house of secrets. My elusive Menabilly … [*author's punctuation*]

The windows were shuttered fast, white and barred. Ivy covered the grey walls and threw tendrils round the windows. The house, like the world, was sleeping too. But later, when the sun was high, there would come no wreath of smoke from the chimneys. The shutters would not be thrown back, or the doors unfastened. No voices would sound within those darkened rooms. Menabilly would sleep on, like the sleeping beauty of the fairy tale, until someone should come to wake her.

Daphne du Maurier 'The House of Secrets' (1946) in *The Rebecca Notebook* (1981), pp.137–138

8b. There was Manderley, our Manderley, secretive and silent as it had always been, the grey stone shining in the moonlight of my dream, the mullioned windows reflecting the green lawns and the terrace. Time could not wreck the perfect symmetry of those walls, nor the site itself, a jewel in the hollow of a hand.

Daphne du Maurier *Rebecca* (1938), Ch.1, p.2

Daphne's Menabilly, on this blithe morning of early summer, is an unthreatening and magical wilderness. There is anticipation as she approaches, tensely creeping towards the open lawn as if she were stalking a shy animal, but no fear. The sun is rising and the dawn chorus provides a fresh accompaniment to her arrival. The house itself seems to catch the light, its windows white, framed by sensitive 'tendrils' of ivy. The list of negatives, which contrasts the uninhabited house with the opening up of an occupied home, suggests the house's potential for life, with open shutters and the sounds of voices. This is a vision of Menabilly in the future, when Daphne and her three children have taken up residence.

The reference to Sleeping Beauty in this passage is hardly needed. We already feel that any intruder in the woods of Menabilly is entering an enchanted realm. By night, a Gothic atmosphere casts a superstitious awe over the trespasser's rational mind, but by day the house seems a benign fairy-tale place, ready for an awakening. Once before, when Daphne made her first passionate vow to Cornwall, 'I for this, and this for me,' she had cast herself in the role of a male lover. Here, before the house of Menabilly, she is the intrepid prince, fighting her way through the impenetrable forest which guards the inner sanctum to claim her beloved.

Though the opening of *Rebecca* is a memorable description of the overgrown drive leading from Four Turnings, just as Daphne and Angela had found it on their very first visit, the house of Menabilly is not the much grander mansion of Manderley. Nonetheless, the reader of *Rebecca*, having followed the dreamer down that twisting path, experiences the same sense of wonder on seeing Manderley that overcame Daphne on her early explorations. Don't forget that when she wrote *Rebecca*, she had only those first illicit visits to feed her imagination. In the novel, her 'elusive Menabilly' becomes 'our Manderley', the house that the narrator had shared with Maxim. Still 'secretive and silent', it seems to have a stronger, almost triumphant presence; this is not a place of dispellable mists and delicate tendrils, but an invulnerable mansion of 'perfect symmetry', its windows glittering like a hard jewel. But once we put the two passages back into context, the significance of the mansions is transformed. It is Manderley in *Rebecca* that is destroyed, and Menabilly where Daphne was to live happily for many years after.

In contrast to Menabilly, there is no softer aspect to Jamaica Inn. Even before we reach the darkened house on the rugged moor, Daphne's readers can be in little doubt that we are being swept away from the reassurance of quotidian realism into the nightmarish world of Gothic romance. Rumours of the 'queer tales' (p.11) that keep respectable folk away from Jamaica Inn wind up the suspense as Mary stands outside the isolated, forbidding house in the black depths of the moor, while the panic-stricken coach driver whips his horses away into the darkness. We have arrived at a house of terror familiar from countless iconic works, whether Horace Walpole's eighteenth-century prototype or the Rocky Horror Show's twentieth-century parody. As the inn door swings open, the fear begins. The man who towers over Mary Yellan, dazzling her with his lantern and pulling her roughly inside the gloomy mansion, is Joss Merlyn – the violent husband of Aunt Patience, the inhospitable landlord of Jamaica Inn, and the blood-stained leader of a ruthless gang of Cornish wreckers.

How does extract 9, opposite, make its impact? Does it put you in mind of any other narratives?

Jamaica Inn stirs up memories of the most potent folk tales of our childhood. Mary Yellan's arrival at its dark doors may recall Jack braving the Giant's lair, or Beauty boldly entering the Beast's castle, seeking a member of her family who has been imprisoned. Or you might have imagined Little Red Riding Hood reaching the safety of her grandmother's cottage to find the Wolf in her bed, his gleaming white fangs all the better to devour the innocent girl in her travelling cloak who has walked into his trap. Joss is also Bluebeard, putting his prohibition on the bloody chamber; Jamaica Inn, as we will shortly discover, has its forbidden room, locked and boarded up, which Mary is naturally determined to enter.

You may have caught some literary echoes in Daphne's description of the remote inn on the moors. This is the harsh terrain of *Wuthering Heights*, and the flagged kitchen where Mary tries to warm her frozen hands at the fire is as unwelcoming as the room that Lockwood reluctantly enters at the opening of Emily Brontë's novel. You might even recall the mistreated canine inhabitants of Heathcliff's hearth when Joss's broken wife, Patience, is described later in Chapter 2 as 'fawning almost, like a whimpering dog that has been trained by constant cruelty' (p.19). Joss, with his 'gypsy' colouring and white teeth like 'the bared fangs of a wolf' is a caricature of Heathcliff himself, who is portrayed

9. Mary stood alone, with the trunk at her feet. She heard a sound of bolts being drawn in the dark house behind her, and the door was flung open. A great figure strode into the yard, swinging a lantern from side to side ...

'Oh, it's you, is it?' he said. 'So you've come to us after all? I'm your uncle, Joss Merlyn, and I bid you welcome to Jamaica Inn.' He drew her into the shelter of the house, laughing again, and shut the door, and stood the lantern upon a table in the passage. And they looked upon each other face to face.

He was a great husk of a man, nearly seven feet high, with a creased black brow and a skin the colour of a gypsy. His thick dark hair fell over his eyes in a fringe and hung about his ears ... The best things left to him were his teeth, which were all good still, and very white, so that when he smiled they showed up clearly against the tan of his face, giving him the lean and hungry appearance of a wolf. And, though there should be a world of difference between the smile of a man and the bared fangs of a wolf, with Joss Merlyn they were one and the same.

Daphne du Maurier *Jamaica Inn* (1936), Ch. 1–2, pp.14–16

The Brontë Legacy

Daphne was proud of her debt to the Brontë sisters. She coined the term 'Gondaling' (after Emily Brontë's fictional kingdom of Gondal) to mean 'imagining', revealing her fascination with the stories woven by the young Brontë sisters and her identification with their need for make-believe. Having immersed herself in the Brontës' fiction as a child, Daphne re-entered the world of Haworth Parsonage when she was invited to write a preface to Wuthering Heights *(Macdonald Classics 1955). This project led her to explore the troubled life of the drug-addicted brother for a full-length biography,* The Infernal World of Branwell Brontë *(1960).*

The Brontë sisters created two of the most famous Gothic houses in English fiction, which cast their shadows over Daphne's early work:

Wuthering Heights

As Mary Yellan approaches Jamaica Inn on Bodmin Moor, many readers will recall the beginning of Emily Brontë's novel, where the narrator reaches the inhospitable farmhouse ruled over by the Byronic figure of Heathcliff. The moors themselves have an extraordinary presence in both novels.

Romance readers may begin to speculate whether Mary Yellan will take after one of Emily Brontë's feisty heroines. Will she turn out like young Catherine, who stands up to Heathcliff's bullying and survives incarceration at the Heights, and if so, can we expect to meet an equivalent to Hareton Earnshaw, Heathcliff's rough young relative, who proves himself to be a suitable match?

Thornfield Hall

Rebecca's earliest readers recognised that Manderley was a tribute to Mr Rochester's mansion in Charlotte Brontë's Jane Eyre. *In both novels, the female narrator's exploration of her large and intimidating new home uncovers a Gothic secret about the master's first wife, who haunts the house – one immured by Rochester, the other murdered by Maxim. The narrators eventually learn how much their taciturn heroes love them. But the rejected wives take their revenge when Thornfield Hall and Manderley go up in flames!*

in *Wuthering Heights* as a dark-skinned gypsy with 'sharp, white teeth', a 'fierce, pitiless, wolfish man.'

You could argue that drawing a parallel with *Wuthering Heights* is too specific, since Emily Brontë's novel is part of a longer tradition of Gothic fiction established well before 1800. Jane Austen, writing forty years before the Brontë sisters picked up their pens, would have had no difficulty in recognising the main features of *Jamaica Inn*, having brilliantly parodied the excesses of popular authors like Mrs Radcliffe in her novel *Northanger Abbey*. The rediscovery of a line of 'female Gothic', spanning two centuries from Radcliffe to *Rebecca*, and on to Angela Carter's *Bloody Chamber*, was the main factor in bringing about Daphne du Maurier's belated appearance on the syllabus of university English departments in the 1990s. But no reader needs a university literature course to understand what is happening in Daphne's contribution to the mainstream of Gothic fiction. In an environment dominated by cruel men, whose threats of physical and psychological violence constantly hang over the women of the house, Mary is the fearful but defiant Gothic heroine, ready to risk the breaking of her body and spirit in her desire to expose the most sinister secrets of Jamaica Inn.

5 *The man in the mirror*

If you look at Daphne's typescript of *The Scapegoat*, which is held in the Special Collections of the University of Exeter, you will see that the novel's original title was 'The Double'. I rather wish that the publishers had kept it, for if I were to pick a theme that best represented the whole body of Daphne's work, this would be the one. Doubles can be found everywhere in Daphne's fiction, and their different uses in *The Scapegoat* and *I'll Never Be Young Again* are the subject of this section.

We have already seen that some of Daphne's heroines feel that their own identity is split – between domesticity and wildness, the cottage and the cliffs. But it is not only women who might be unsettled, aware of a part of themselves that remains unsatisfied. In *Gerald*, Daphne's perceptive biography of her father, she describes his 'odd little demon of restlessness', which he may have inherited from her grandfather, the artist George du Maurier. 'Was there something in the blood,' she asks, 'that made them both long for the infinite and be for ever unappeased?' (p.114). If there was, she might have added, it was a demon of restlessness that she had inherited within herself.

Her fictional men are particularly prone to repressing more vibrant or vicious inner selves, while presenting a reserved exterior to their acquaintances. The scholarly English narrator of *The Scapegoat*, 'a law-abiding, quiet, donnish individual of thirty-eight,' is a classic du Maurier anti-hero. Driving homewards at the end of his vacation in France, dissatisfied with himself and his life, he chances to stop off at a bar and has a life-changing opportunity to explore 'the self who clamoured for release, the man within.'

Please read the two extracts opposite,10a and 10b, from the opening chapters of *The Scapegoat* where John meets Jean. Do they strike you as two men, or one?

10a. … I lived and breathed and had my being as a law-abiding, quiet, donnish individual of thirty-eight. But to the self who clamoured for release, the man within? How did my poor record seem to him?

Who he was and whence he sprang, what urges and what longings he might possess, I could not tell. I was so used to denying him expression that his ways were unknown to me … Perhaps, if I had not kept him locked within me, he might have laughed, roistered, fought and lied.

Daphne du Maurier *The Scapegoat* (1957), Ch. 1, pp.6–7

10b. Someone jolted my elbow as I drank and said, 'Je vous demande pardon,' and as I moved to give him space he turned and stared at me and I at him, and I realized, with a strange sense of shock and fear and nausea all combined, that his face and voice were known to me too well.

I was looking at myself …

He took me by the arm and pulled me closer to the counter, and although the mirror behind the bar was steamy, and partly hidden by glasses and bottles, and confusing because of the many reflections of the other heads, it showed us plainly enough to be standing together, straining, anxious, searching the mirrored surface as though our lives depended upon what it had to tell. And the answer was no chance resemblance, no superficial likeness to be confounded by the different colour of hair or eyes, by the dissimilarity of feature, expression, height, or breadth of shoulder: it was as though one man stood there …

We might have been two actors studying our make-up as we glanced from the looking-glass back to one another.

Daphne du Maurier *The Scapegoat* (1957), Ch. 1–2, pp.9–11

On one level, the plot of *The Scapegoat* takes literally the idea of an alter ego. There are two men standing here, who turn out to be different in rather significant ways, and readers have to suppress their disbelief that only their blood groups – and their behaviour as lovers – allow others to distinguish between them. But of course Jean de Gué, with his demanding family ties, his mistress, and his dubious morals, is also the man John might have been, the self who would have 'laughed, roistered, fought and lied.'

It is no accident that there is a mysteriously steamy mirror behind the bar in which the two men can study their own reflections. Looking in a mirror and seeing your other self is a Gothic trick that Daphne uses on many occasions. At the end of her story 'Not After Midnight', for example, the introverted male narrator, who has so far managed to keep the vices of his inner self within bounds, looks down into the sea from a boat; he thinks that what he sees are the eyes of a drowned man staring up at him – or is it a deceptive reflection, a premonition of his own future when he will look in a mirror and see that the drink-sodden face has become his own? In the bar scene of *The Scapegoat*, it is not their difference that fascinates the two men, as they gaze at their images in the mirror, but their extraordinary superficial likeness. Only they know that the similarity is skin-deep. How deep the differences might be is what John, returning to Jean de Gué's chateau in the clothes of his double, is ready to discover.

Perhaps the most notorious case of a split character in English literature is found in Robert Louis Stevenson's *Dr Jekyll and Mr Hyde* – a novella which also has an important central scene with a looking glass, when the distinguished Dr Jekyll first examines his dramatically changed appearance in the form of his repellently ugly inner persona, Mr Hyde. We therefore think of alter egos as representing the voracious id within us all – demanding, sexual, selfish, cruel – which for the sake of civilised society we learn to keep in check. Daphne certainly took this line, especially in her darkest short stories. But this was not always the function of the 'other' or mirrored self. Many of her men, like John in *The Scapegoat*, may be starving the more generous and emotional side of their nature, and missing out on the better half of life.

Daphne was equally fascinated by characters at odds with a more ascetic self, the spiritual element of our being which always intrigued her. At its simplest, this 'soulful' self is represented by a monastic existence: at the end of *The Scapegoat*, John is still not reconciled to his previous academic life, but heads for the silence of the Cistercian monastery that was drawing him at the start of the story. It is an option that attracted other characters in her work. In the story 'Monte Verità', discussed later in Part 3, the beautiful heroine chooses self-denial and retreat to the mountains. Even in the draft of *Rebecca*, in a passage expunged in the typescript sent to the publishers, the young narrator gives Maxim an additional piece of information about her father, who left his family to become a monk. It is a telling detail, finally omitted from the novel as we have it, which would certainly have led the reader down a new line of speculation about the psychology of the daughter, and her behaviour as the second Mrs de Winter!

Daphne's work taken as a whole suggests that we are all in some ways split selves – or more accurately multiple selves, some good, some bad – and that it is unusual, probably inadvisable, perhaps impossible, to live a life that allows expression to our inner demons and dark doubles. Only in a fictional world like that of *The Scapegoat* can a character consider giving full rein to his alter ego, and only through reading such narratives can we begin to imagine what such a process might entail.

I'll Never Be Young Again, Daphne du Maurier's second novel, also plays with the idea of the double, though it is very different in approach from *The Scapegoat* (and indeed astonishingly different in its new form and modern subject matter from her first book, *The Loving Spirit*). The narrator is a young man, depressed to the point of suicide by his upbringing: though Dick had a privileged childhood in material terms, his self-belief was systematically undermined by his gifted father. At the end of Chapter One, Dick is bent on drowning himself in the Thames, and only a few seconds away from letting go.

Please read extract 11 overleaf. Are there any clues here as to the type of person Jake will turn out to be?

Since Dick tells us this is when he saw Jake for the first time, we realise that he is intended to be a continuing feature of the story, and indeed without Jake there would be no more story to tell or narrator to tell it. Our image is immediately positive, of a man offering security, a man with 'a smile on his lips' – that is, a very different person from the anxious youth whose fate we have been following through the previous pages. Yet Jake turns out to be a curious presence in the novel, hardly a character at all. You could regard this as a flaw

11. I swung my legs over, holding on to the bridge with desperate fingers. An odd snatch of breeze blew across my hair. I supposed that this was the very last thing of the world to come to me.

I breathed deeply, and I felt as though the waiting water rose up in front of me and would not let me go.

This was my final impression of horror, when fear and fascination took hold upon me, and I knew that I should have no other moment but this before the river itself closed in upon me. My fingers slackened, and I lowered myself for the fall.

It was then that someone laid his hands upon my shoulder, and turning to clutch him instinctively as a means of safety, I saw Jake for the first time, his head thrown back, a smile on his lips.

'You don't want to do that,' he said …

Daphne du Maurier *I'll Never be Young Again* (1932), Ch. 1–2, pp.8–9 in an essentially realist work – Dick's relationship with a woman in the second half of this book is more vivid and three-dimensional – or you could be as curious as I am about Daphne's experimentation with this shape-changing figure, whose purpose seems to shift page by page. When Jake makes his first, life-saving intervention in Dick's life, he is a kind of inner double, thrown up by Dick's survival instinct to protect him. He takes Dick off on an adventurous voyage to escape from his old life – 'We'll get away in a ship together, you and I' (p.15) – and then on a series of journeys that enable Dick to grow up. When he plans to take Dick into the mountains, the men have one of those strange long exchanges – more like a film script than a descriptive novel – that characterise the first half of the book. Here are some extracts:

> 'I'll get the horrors, Jake, in these hills. They're too big for me.'
> 'You won't be alone.' …
> 'I wish I was different.'
> 'You're all right.' …
> 'I wish I could write like my father.'
> 'You could if you wanted.'
> 'No, I couldn't, Jake. I'm only an ordinary fellow without any guts.'
> 'You don't train yourself. You don't know about discipline. There's a whole lot of you that you're too lazy to bring out.' …
> 'This is big enough, anyway.'
> 'There won't always be this.'
> 'You won't chuck me, Jake?'
> 'No.' (Ch. 6, pp.46–48)

Who Jake is, and how he feels, are hidden from us. What comes across is Dick's neediness, his use of Jake to fill the place of a father figure/ teacher/ guide, and also the place of a mother/ lover, someone to provide unconditional support and understanding. In other words, Jake is all the people we need to help us become psychologically strong and independent adults.

When Dick finds himself, at the dramatic close of Part One, cast into the seas in a shipwreck and facing the death he had once planned for himself, he has a glimpse – or a vision – of Jake, 'his head flung back and his smile' (p.139). And this time Dick survives without Jake, who is no longer needed and therefore disappears from his life forever. Jake is not so much a double, then, as a personification of the forces within the psyche of an individual that keep us surviving and growing.

There is, additionally, another kind of doubling at work in this book. As Margaret Forster argues in her biography, Dick is an alter ego for Daphne herself. He is 21 when the novel begins, the age Daphne had been when she met the film director Carol Reed, with whom she was having her first affair as she wrote the book. Many of Dick's uncertainties, his naïve theorising about life, his same-sex dependence on an older friend, his attempts to grasp a better comprehension of the adult world, may represent aspects of the way in which Daphne saw her slightly younger self. But in her exploration of his sexuality through a relationship with a young woman in Part Two, she may also have projected something of herself into Dick's lover, so splitting herself across the two elements in this couple.

This type of speculation does not necessarily give us any definite biographical insights, nor am I suggesting that learning more about the author would be the purpose of reading the novel. What it does show, though, is the complex function of characters in fiction, who do not need to be rounded and credible to tell us truths about the nature of personal identity, and the multi-dimensional lives we all live.

6 Family dramas

The forces that drive Daphne's fictional families are volatile, even volcanic. Her obsession with the darker side of life leads her to explore the underlying rivalries and primitive passions that can erupt into the daily life of a family with devastating consequences. We can find traces of this theme throughout her writing, but nowhere is the impact of family dysfunction more disturbing than in her early novel, *Julius*.

Daphne's third book, which she completed when she was only 26, is staggeringly accomplished in its style and scope. Recording the life of a dynamic French Jew from birth to death, it follows ambitiously in the tradition of nineteenth-century French realist fiction. Part One, Julius's childhood, encompasses his dirty, crowded birthplace, the colourful market where his peasant grandfather sold cheeses from a stall, the Prussian invasion that turned the family into refugees in a Paris under siege, and the return of Julius's Jewish father to Algeria, where he died and left Julius to be educated at the synagogue. But such a summary does not do justice to the vigour and rawness of this novel. As a child, Julius witnessed his first murder, when his father strangled his mother for adultery. This death in Part One is not the last: another almost random killing of an Arab merchant, hit by a catapult and robbed of his mules, takes place only a few pages into Part Two. The continuing tension of the book, bound up with Julius's callousness about sexual relationships and his ruthlessness in pursuit of wealth, holds the reader's horrified fascination. Once your father has brutally murdered your mother, your future life must surely hold more suffering and violence.

Please read extract 12a, overleaf, to the phrase 'It was Gabriel', where Part Three of the novel ends.

12a. [Julius] looked into the room and he saw her standing by the window with the flute to her lips, watching the white clouds pass across the sky. She raised herself on tiptoe as though by drawing herself up she could throw the notes into the air, as though she would break the silence, disturb and torture the dumbness of the dark room.

Her curls were brushed behind her ears, forming a clump at the back of her neck, golden and thick. Impatient and careless, she tapped with her foot upon the floor.

Disturbed by the opening door she turned, and then flung a smile over her shoulder, her eyes watching his eyes.

Julius did not smile back; he looked at her, her face, her body, her hands on the flute, the colour of her hair; he looked at her figure outlined against the window, and a fierce sharp joy came to him stronger than any known sensation, something primitive like the lick of a flame and the first taste of blood, as though a message ran through his brain saying: 'I for this – and this for me.'

It was Gabriel.

Daphne du Maurier *Julius* (1933), Part Three, p.213

What do you think the relationship is between the girl (Gabriel) and the man who is looking at her (Julius)?
Only after thinking about 12a, continue with 12b, below. How do you feel when you read on?

12b. He was fifty, his body and his mind were undergoing some organic chemical change – he needed a tonic. So here was Gabriel at fifteen, with an abundance of youth and health and vitality which she must give to him because she belonged ...

He had brought her into the world and now he was ready for her.

This voracious passion for his daughter that started so swiftly was like a match giving blaze to a high explosive; only the explosive burnt up and around, stretching farther and beyond with flaming tentacles, and was not extinguished.

Daphne du Maurier *Julius* (1933), Part Four, p.217–218

I am sure every reader reacted with shock on realising that Julius's passion is for his own daughter. He is 50, she is 15. The description of Gabriel through his eyes is of a Spirit of Youth, playing her grandfather's flute like a Greek nymph or a carefree Pan, and bringing the freshness of nature, the white clouds in the sky, into the darkness of the house. But Julius's feelings for Gabriel are far from innocent. There is an erotic charge around the description of his daughter's abundant hair, the 'golden and thick' curls at the back of her neck. We become uncomfortably aware that we are following Julius's gaze as he runs his eyes over 'her face, her body, her hands ... '

Daphne delighted in breaking taboos in her writing, unafraid to explore sexual deviance, murderous desires, and the dysfunctional family, or in some cases, all three together. The greatest taboo for most cultures is incest – sexual connection between brothers and sisters, or parents and children – a recurring theme in Daphne's work. Her most explicit incest plot can be found in the story 'A Border-line Case' (1971), where a young actress seeks out a friend of her father's, an IRA man. 'I think I must have loved you without knowing it all my life,' the heroine confesses (p.154). Her instinct is explained when her lover turns out – after a brief intense affair – to be her biological father.

Daphne had experienced the possessiveness of a father in her own relationship with Gerald, but in Julius she took the passion to its greatest extreme. Gabriel's father sees her youthfulness as a source of renewed vitality in middle age, giving him a 'taste of blood' as if he were a vampire seeking fresh prey. The selfishness of his 'voracious passion' is only too evident. But the primitive emotions ignited by his newly sexualised awareness of his teenage daughter are real and violent enough, so violent that they can lead only to tragedy. The tremendous redefinition of the father/ daughter dynamic in this scene has more than enough power to drive the rest of the novel to its dramatic conclusion.

My Cousin Rachel has undercurrents that are almost as disturbing as incest. We have already seen how the ghoulish corpse in the opening pages clouds the story-telling with the narrator's guilt (discussed at the end of Section 3 pp.37–38). Philip has been taken to see the shocking sight by his uncle,

Ambrose Ashley, as part of his education in the ways of the world, and these pages are also the place where Ambrose's paternal relationship to his heir is established. 'As my guardian, father, brother, counsellor, as in fact my whole world,' writes his nephew, 'he was forever testing me' (p.1). Philip freely admits to having idolised his uncle, and turning the clock forward eighteen years, he realises: 'I have become so like him that I might be his ghost ... The man who whistled to his dogs and turned his back upon the four roads and the gibbet could be myself. Well, it was what I always wanted. To be like him' (p.4).

As a gauche young man, Philip travels to Italy to visit Ambrose and his new Italian wife Rachel at their villa, only to find that Ambrose has died in mysterious circumstances. Suspicious and jealous, Philip does not at first welcome the widow's visit to their Cornish estate, but slowly her presence works the same enchantment on him as it had on Ambrose. His view of Rachel perpetually fluctuates between adoration and desperation: by Chapter 20, he sees her as an insidious femme fatale (a passage analysed in Section 3 pp.36–37). The extract we are now going to consider falls at an earlier stage in their relationship, when Philip is only beginning to feel the disturbing influence on his emotions that will cause him to fall in love with her.

Please read extract 13 overleaf. How do Rachel's words prepare the reader for what will happen later?

What further interpretation could be put on the Ambrose/Rachel/Philip triangle?

The telling pause at the end of the dinner-table scene primes us for a significant response from Rachel. It is becoming obvious to the reader, if not to Philip himself, that he is vulnerable to his cousin's charms, and the reminder that she is, by virtue of being Ambrose's widow, already 'Mrs Ashley' hints at the possibility that she might in the future become Mrs Philip Ashley, and the rightful hostess at his dinner table. In other words, we are aware that history could be repeating itself – and that Rachel would then have found another way of coming into ownership of Ambrose's Cornish estate. For, though Philip is still grieving for his uncle and wishing that he could be with them, he is now the heir sitting in Ambrose's place at the head of the table.

The parallels between Ambrose and Philip in their relationship with Rachel are set to become even more intriguing. Will Philip also end by

13. When we had finished dessert, and the port was put upon the table, I did not know whether I should rise, as I usually did, to open the door, or if, now I had a hostess opposite me, it would be [Rachel's] place to give some signal. There was a pause in the conversation. Suddenly she looked at me and smiled. I smiled back at her in answer. We seemed to hold each other for a moment. It was queer, strange. The feeling went right through me, never before known.

Then my godfather remarked in his gruff deep voice, 'Tell me, Mrs Ashley, does not Philip remind you very much of Ambrose?'

There was a moment's silence. She put down her napkin on the table. 'So much so,' she said, 'that I have wondered, sitting here at dinner, if there is any difference.'

Daphne du Maurier *My Cousin Rachel* (1951), Ch. 11, p.119

anguishing about 'Rachel, my torment', as Ambrose had once expressed his agony in one of his last notes home? But the reader may uneasily sense that there is something else wrong here, something improper about Philip embarking on an affair with Rachel, whether he marries her or not. This is getting close to a family taboo, though a man could not be legally at fault by sleeping with his dead uncle's widow.

The Victorians had recognised a similarly charged relationship in repeatedly debating but failing to repeal the Deceased Wife's Sister's Act of 1835, which prevented a man from marrying his sister-in-law. There are practical considerations that might apply here, since in the nineteenth century single women might well live with a married sister as part of the household, and find themselves in a delicate situation if the sister died. At least they could not be accused of husband-hunting, once the possibility of marrying their sister's widower was legally removed, and the barrier might also put them out of temptation's way from the point of view of their brother-in-law, allowing them to stay on in the domestic establishment in the respectable role of housekeeper. But what was really at stake, as the obsession with the theme in a number of Victorian novels makes clear, was the whiff of incest that clung to such unions, despite the absence of a blood relationship between the spouses. A similar objection attaches itself to Philip's desire to marry Rachel, and to the clandestine nights he spends with her.

At a deeper level, an even stronger Freudian prohibition asserts itself. For Ambrose is effectively Philip's father, and Philip is therefore symbolically re-enacting the ancient sin embedded in every boy's psyche (according to Sigmund Freud) of wanting to kill his father in order to marry his mother. Ambrose has conveniently died before Philip meets Rachel – or did she poison him and thus inadvertently make way for his brother? Is the guilt that saturates this novel a symptom not of Philip's murderous suspicion of Rachel as a poisoner, but of his knowledge that he himself would have wanted to kill Ambrose in order to marry Rachel, and is indeed proposing to benefit from his murder?

If you are blanching at this theory, think for a moment of *Hamlet*, discussed by Freud in *The Interpretation of Dreams* (1900). The troubled prince was exercised about a similar problem, even closer to the Freudian paradigm, when he discovered that his uncle had poisoned his father. Not only had his uncle thereby usurped the kingdom of Denmark; he had enabled himself to marry Hamlet's mother, who willingly entered her brother-in-law's bed and thus unwittingly conspired with her husband's murder. Could Hamlet's feelings of guilt and his inability to take revenge on his uncle be due to his own unadmitted desire to sleep with his mother in his uncle's place? Had he murdered his own father in his heart? No wonder the Prince of Denmark is no more able than Philip Ashley to come to any decisions about the culpability of others and how he should act. In both works, the suppressed guilt of this original sin spreads through the plot like a noxious miasma that can never be dispelled.

Daphne explores guilt to terrific effect in book after book. The sense that we are all by nature guilty of some terrible crime, or of the potential to commit some crime, pervades a surprising amount of her work. The most murderous impulses of all emerge from the core of the family, and from the magnification of feelings that everyone has experienced. We shall be meeting this theme again in the discussion of other du Maurier works later in this book.

7 *Tourist, tripper, spender, spy*

Daphne was always vexed by the summer intrusion of tourists and holiday makers into her personal corner of Cornwall, but her response went far beyond annoyance at the litter and the visitors' lack of respect for rural quiet to encompass more unsettling implications of tourism as a modern phenomenon. In *Vanishing Cornwall* (1967, new edition 2007), which involved her in serious research on the region's history and politics, she wrote vehemently against Cornwall's adoption of tourism as an economic panacea. Her unbridled rhetoric on the topic was somewhat tamed by her editors before *Vanishing Cornwall's* publication, and it wasn't until her last novel, *Rule Britannia* (1972), that she took the opportunity to let rip.

The plot is based on the fantasy of an American occupation of Britain, and in the extract overleaf the elderly heroine, who lives like Daphne in a Cornish coastal area bordering on the clay-mining district near Par, is reading about US plans to turn the whole of the UK into a theme park for the benefit of global tourists.

How does Daphne du Maurier make her point in extract 14?

This crude exaggeration of the American scheme for Britain is typical of *Rule Britannia's* often heavy-handed satire. Not content with generalising about new ways of catering for the modern tourist, Daphne piles on ridiculous examples of historical re-enactment – even the resurrection of blood sports like bear-baiting and cock-fighting for the entertainment of the passive consumer in his car. The book develops a parallel between the invasion of Britain by the US navy and the serious threat to national and regional culture that Daphne saw in the Americanisation and 'touristification' of the country. She feared

14. Plans for Great Britain herself [as part of the new USUK alliance] would take some little time to formulate. It must be recognised that her heyday as a great industrial nation had now ended, but a new future lay ahead for her as the historical and cultural centre of the English-speaking peoples ... The scope was literally tremendous. 'There is not a county in England or Wales,' wrote an enthusiastic supporter of the scheme, 'that is not steeped in history ... Hotels and restaurants could be transformed into old coaching inns ... Bear-baiting, cock-fighting, jousting, duelling, masked highwaymen on horseback – the tourist could watch them all from the comfort of a roofed-in stadium, or even from his car.'

Daphne du Maurier *Rule Britannia* (1972), Ch. 11, pp.136–137 that the pre-war Cornwall she loved was vanishing under economic pressures that would lead to a wave of over-development and tourist expansion, and that planners would not have the imagination to resist the despoiling of the landscape and the cheapening of Cornish culture. In the memorable title of a later TV documentary on the subject, which became a local catch-phrase, Cornwall faced a future of 'concrete and cream teas', and Daphne's voice has been only one of many raised in concern over the past fifty years.

Rule Britannia quotes an invented local newspaper editorial, which applies American-led policy to Cornwall:

> *Our partners from across the Atlantic have pointed out that the Cornish china clay industry is on the decline. Therefore we must turn to tourism in a far more concentrated way. (Ch.11, p.137)*

This is hardly satire – it is too close to actuality to be funny! The need to forge a more robust future for the region than can be delivered by seasonal tourism, which services visitors' leisure requirements with insufficient regard to the basic needs of Cornwall, was so apparent to Daphne that she even allowed herself to be drawn into local politics. As an incomer, and a very private person, she had always remained detached, but in 1969 – though not without some amusement on her part at her unwonted display of commitment – she accepted an invitation to join the Cornish nationalist party, Mebyon Kernow.

Mebyon Kernow and Cornish Identity

Throughout the 20th century, Cornwall has expressed in numerous ways its sense of difference from England, and its affinity with the Celtic regions of Brittany, Wales and Scotland. The nationalistic thinking of the group Mebyon Kernow at its high point in the 1960s is reflected in Daphne du Maurier's Vanishing Cornwall *and her last novel* Rule Britannia.

The Celtic revival of the early 20th century

The Celtic-Cornish Society, founded in 1901, encourages historical research and the revival of the Cornish language (last spoken in the 18th century). The first Gorsedd, Cornwall's version of the Welsh Eisteddford, is held in 1928. Old Cornwall Societies are established, still active in many villages today.

The Rise of Mebyon Kernow

1951 *Mebyon Kernow ('Sons of Cornwall') founded*

1960s *MK attracts growing support from local people and incomers as a pro-Cornwall pressure group, especially in its resistance to an unpopular plan to relocate Greater London overspill populations in Cornwall*

1968 *MK publishes* What Cornishmen Can Do, *a pamphlet setting out options for a viable local economy*

1968 *Membership reaches 1000*

1969 *Daphne du Maurier agrees to join MK, and writes an article for MK's magazine* Cornish Nation *under the headline 'Stand On Your Own Two Feet', which advocates a 'form of self-government' for Cornwall*

1970 *MK puts up its own parliamentary candidate, in the hope of mirroring the success of the Welsh and Scottish nationalists (though by this date a resurgent Liberal Party in Cornwall has adopted many of MK's pro-Cornish aims)*

Vanishing Cornwall *(1967)*

Despite her tart criticism of the more ambitious and romantic aims of the nationalists, Daphne's overwhelmingly loyal account of Cornwall's past and present raises serious issues about Cornwall's identity and its economic prospects that show a strong affinity with MK's agenda.

Rule Britannia *(1972)*

In the crazily improbable plot of Rule Britannia, *a Cornish resistance movement defeats a US plan to run Britain. The novel's cast includes a Welsh beachcomber named Taffy as a humorous tribute to vague Cornish hopes for a pan-Celtic alliance. Underlying the farcical elements of the book is the clear intention to reject Westminster's patronising attitude to the Cornish periphery, and affirm solidarity with the indigenous farmers, fishermen and clay workers who represent pride in Cornish difference.*

Daphne's Cornish novels tend to use tourism to highlight the ugliness and artificiality of the modern world, thereby magnifying the allure of the past. In *The House on the Strand*, bathing huts line the Cornish sands 'like dentures in an open mouth.' In the evocative opening chapter of *Frenchman's Creek*, the River Helford's romantic history is provocatively glimpsed in the shadows of the vulgar present, when summer days are crowded with pleasure steamers, leisure yachtsmen and day trippers. Even in pre-war *Rebecca*, holiday-makers threaten the margins of Manderley, not only with the litter and noise that Daphne detested but also with their degrading lack of appreciation of the landscape.

In the episode of *Rebecca* where the steamer runs onto the rocks in the fog, holiday-makers flock to the scene, and one of the visitors strikes up a conversation with Maxims's wife on the cliff path.

In extract 15, overleaf, how is the reader being encouraged to react to the woman in the pink striped frock?

Compared to the shrinking Mrs de Winter, the holiday-maker comes across as warm and friendly. But she is surely intended to sound slightly common, a little too chatty, and only too ready to see the shipwreck as an additional excitement for the benefit of visitors. Someone who overuses the word 'nice' – teachers used to underline 'nice' and demand a more interesting synonym – is being tagged as lower middle class. And phrases like 'lovely spot' and 'nice-looking woods' are not the language of anyone deemed to be sufficiently responsive to the beauty of the coast and the Manderley estate. The greater underlying threat is that the philistines with their petit-bourgeois demand for bungalows will take over in time, and the peace of places like Manderley, sympathetically managed for centuries by the gentry-led social order, will be lost, not just for the summer months but for ever.

The problem, in Daphne's view, extended far beyond the West Country: in her vision of the twentieth century, tourism was ruining the whole of Europe. Even peasants in the smallest hamlets and travellers seeking solitude in the wilderness were no longer safe. In 'Monte Verità', a story which depends on the remoteness of the mountains where a religious cult has its magnificent monastic retreat, the narrator muses that today there may be 'resting camps near the summit, even an hotel in the little village on the eastern slopes, and the tourist lifted to the twin peaks by electric cable' (p.43). Daphne's novels and stories are laced with such despairing references to tourism, which had become for her something of an obsession.

15. A woman in a pink striped frock and a hair-net came across the grass towards us ... She was a holiday-maker from Kerrith ...

'It's a lovely spot up here, isn't it?' she said to me. 'We brought a picnic lunch, never thinking it would turn foggy and we'd have a wreck into the bargain ...'

'Those are nice-looking woods over there; I suppose they're private,' said the woman ... 'My husband says all these big estates will be chopped up in time and bungalows built ... I wouldn't mind a nice little bungalow up here facing the sea. I don't know that I'd care for this part of the world in the winter though.'

Daphne du Maurier *Rebecca* (1938), Ch. 19, pp.287–288

Yet Daphne was herself an experienced European traveller, who got to know France as a teenager, enjoyed ski-ing parties and cosmopolitan café culture as a young woman, met up with family and friends for city breaks in Florence and Venice, and latterly took Mediterranean holidays with her grown-up children. Trips to Urbino and Crete with her son and daughter-in-law inspired *The Flight of the Falcon* and 'Not After Midnight', and incidents on a visit to Venice with her daughter Tessa sowed the seeds of 'Don't Look Now'. No innocent abroad, she recognised that she was behaving in the same way as the visitors she resented in her beloved Cornwall, and it did not escape her that authors in particular were as culpable as tourists in the self-centred way that they observed other communities for their own purposes. She describes in the preface to one of her collections of short stories how, as a young writer, she found that 'something observed, something said,' as she sat in a Parisian café or with a French friend, provided the seed for a later story ('The Rendezvous', p.xiii). Writers are voyeurs, always watching other people and mentally storing away material for future use. In this respect, Daphne has to admit, they are not unlike tourists with their insatiable thirst for new cultural experiences to be recounted on postcards and captured by their ever-ready cameras.

Some of her later stories play amusingly on tourist behaviour. 'The Way of the Cross' is a discomfiting account of the embarrassments suffered by a group of English pilgrims on an excursion to Jerusalem. The party fragments as the individuals come to grief in different farcical ways – Lady Althea's capped front teeth fall out, the honeymoon couple fall foul of a predatory husband, and the minister gets tummy trouble. The tribulations of a tour guide are expanded on at much greater length in *The Flight of the Falcon*, in which the Italian narrator is a courier of English and American visitors (known in the tourist trade as Beef and Barbarians). 'Don't Look Now' is more subtle, opening with a scene of a couple on holiday making fun of other tourists; part of the holiday spectacle is the 'other' visitors, generally considered to be less sophisticated than ourselves. The couple are prepared to take jokes to an extreme, envisaging the two respectable elderly ladies at the next table as male twins in drag, 'doing the sights of Europe, changing sex at each stop.' When it emerges that one of the women is blind and can't look now, it is time for the tasteless mockery to stop, but already too late. Events in this fast-paced plot have moved on, and the idea of 'looking' has gone beyond the intrusive tourist gaze to the phenomenon of 'second sight' and the fatal pursuit of a figure wrongly 'seen' as a lost child.

An equally clever play on the notion of tourists as voyeurs is entwined

16a. I was shown a brochure which seemed to meet my requirements. A pleasantly situated hotel close to the sea, and chalets by the water's edge where one slept and breakfasted. Clientèle well-to-do, and although I count myself no snob I cannot abide paper-bags and orange-peel.

Daphne du Maurier 'Not After Midnight' (1971), p.58

16b. I stacked away my [painting] gear, and … watched a motor-boat with gently purring engine draw in softly to the eastward point with the landing-stage away to my right … Then all three [people aboard] stared in my direction, and the second man, who had been standing in the stern, put up a pair of binoculars and fixed them on me. He held them steady for several minutes, focusing, no doubt, on every detail of my personal appearance, which is unremarkable enough, heaven knows, and would have continued had I not suddenly become annoyed and withdrawn into the bedroom, slamming the shutters to.

Daphne du Maurier 'Not After Midnight' (1971), pp.63–64

through the sinister story 'Not After Midnight'. The narrator is another of du Maurier's inadequate men, one Timothy Grey, a prep school teacher with 'an aversion to becoming involved with people' (p.57), who goes on a painting holiday in Crete.

What does extract 16a, opposite, tell you about the character of the narrator? What causes the frisson of uneasiness in extract 16b?

The rather reserved language – the formality of 'requirements' and the moderation of 'pleasantly situated' – is entirely in keeping with the self-portrait already drawn for us by formal, almost prim, Mr Grey. He may deny snobbery, but his polite shrinking from the 'paper-bags and orange-peel' of the lower-class holiday maker, however close to the author's own instincts, is imbued with a patronising, old-fashioned fastidiousness ('I cannot abide ...'). He reacts defensively when his instinct for privacy is compromised by the behaviour of other visitors, who gaze at him through their binoculars as if he were another species of local fauna (16b). The intrusive flash of those field glasses punctuates the story, and the sight of a snorkel pipe, probing the water below his chalet that night 'like a minute periscope' (p.68) is another intrusion on his retreat. Both incidents are attributed to the strange motives of the American couple in the next chalet. Spying and counter-espionage become an emerging motif of the narrative, as Grey drives after the couple into the tourist town. He spends an evening ostensibly sitting in a café on the harbour, 'savouring what is known as "local colour", amused by the passing crowd' (p.73). Indistinguishable in his behaviour from other tourists like himself, he is actually on the watch for the mysterious, possibly murderous fellow guests from his hotel. The reader cannot miss the clear parallels between normal tourist behaviour and an unscrupulous interest in other people's business.

Daphne du Maurier's writing, then, explores a wide gamut of themes relating to tourism, as she contrasts the self-righteous superiority of the sensitive incomer or discriminating traveller with the crassness of the mere tourist or tripper. She presents objectionable characters, whose staring and spying throw the tourist project into question, but she self-consciously adds herself, and other writers, to their number. Is it morally right, let alone ultimately beneficial to those places and peoples under scrutiny from those café-watchers, camera-wavers, and consumers of other people's culture, to play the tourist role? We come away from Daphne's stories squirming at the thought of our own holiday selves.

8 *The world's a stage*

'*Peter Pan* was practically our birthright,' wrote Daphne's elder sister Angela, who was to have the magical opportunity in her twenties of playing the part of Wendy on stage:

> *Indeed we were related to the Boy, and its author was one's Uncle Jim. … Barrie used to visit us in our nursery and we used to act it for him by the hour. Daphne always bagged Peter …*
>
> (Angela du Maurier *It's Only The Sister*, pp.14–15)

The story of Captain Hook and the Lost Boys sank deep into Daphne's imagination, where it merged with adventure books like *Treasure Island* and *The Wreck of the Grosvenor*. Peter's insolent provocation of Hook is displayed by Dona St Columb, playing her breeches part in *Frenchman's Creek*, when she recklessly joins the pirate raid on Fowey to capture the Rashleighs' ship and Godolphin's wig. Daphne's own lifelong readiness to identify with Peter is as apparent in her last novel, *Rule Britannia*, as it was in her unpublished teenage tales.

The surreal story of *Rule Britannia*, briefly introduced in the last section, is set in the very real neighbourhood of Daphne's last home, Kilmarth. The heroine is an eighty-year-old eccentric actress, known as Mad, who has adopted six unruly children – Barrie's Lost Boys in modern dress. Cornwall is being invaded by the Americans in the name of a new political alliance between the US and UK (or USUK), which masks an attempted American occupation of Britain.

In an early scene, before the significance of the droning planes and local roadblocks becomes clear, Mad's granddaughter Emma finds one of the boys playing with a bow and arrows on the roof.

What connection do you see between *Peter Pan* and the incident described in extract 17a, overleaf? What role is Mad playing in extract 17b?

How seriously do you think the reader should be taking this novel?

The first extract occurs in the opening chapter of the novel, when the reader's antennae are at full stretch, alert for signals that indicate the genre of the narrative and therefore tell us how to take the following pages. Daphne is obviously aiming for humour – never her best suit – both in Andy's childish pot-shot at the helicopters and in the discrepancy between Mad's account of her bow collection and her son's put-down. Our uneasiness at how we should

Peter Pan

J.M. Barrie created the game of Peter Pan and the pirates for boys he met in Kensington Gardens and later adopted. The five Llewelyn Davies brothers were Daphne's cousins. Barrie (Uncle Jim) watched performances of Peter Pan *in the du Maurier nursery, in which Daphne always took the role of Peter, while her elder sister Angela was Wendy and her younger sister Jeanne gallantly acted the rest of the parts. In the 1920s, a grown-up Angela played Wendy for three seasons on the London stage.*

Gerald du Maurier, Daphne's famous father, was the definitive Captain Hook. He took on the role many times (often combining it with the part of Mr Darling) from the first production of Peter Pan *in 1904. Reviewing a revival in 1929,* The Times *applauded: 'What a moment it was for those with long memories ... when the hornpipe was stepped again with the old dainty diablerie ... There have been so many excellent Hooks, yet only one Hook, and this is the one.'*

Gladys Cooper, one of Gerald's best-known leading ladies during the 1920s and 1930s, twice played the part of Peter. At the age of 81, still acting, she became the inspiration behind Daphne's last novel, Rule Britannia *(1972), which has an eccentric retired actress as its heroine and a Peter Pan theme.*

17a. How on earth, Emma wondered, had Andy managed not only to climb the dangerous sloping roof but to carry with him one of the bows which all the boys were forbidden to touch, and which should by rights be standing with its fellows in the entrance-hall?

'Given me by a field-marshal,' Mad [Emma's grandmother] used to say. 'Toxophily was his favourite hobby. He was one of my greatest fans for years.'

'Completely untrue,' Pa would whisper to Emma. 'She brought them at the Battersea fun-fair.'

True or false, the arrows that went with the bows were lethal. Andy's head and shoulders emerged from the chimney. He smiled engagingly at Emma.

'I only grazed the pigeon,' he called. 'I didn't mean to, I wanted to scare the aircraft, but they were out of my range. Several choppers came low, and if they'd only been a few hundred feet lower I might have got one of the pilots.'

Daphne du Maurier *Rule Britannia* (1972), Ch. 1, pp.8–9

17b. Emma glanced nervously at her grandmother. At least she hadn't got her peaked cap on ... Actually, with her white hair brushed upwards like that she looked rather good. Formidable, in fact. On the other hand, it might have been better if she had been dressed to suit her near-eighty years, perhaps in a sensible skirt, and worn a soft cardigan around her shoulders, preferably pale blue, instead of that Robin Hood jerkin with leather sleeves.

Daphne du Maurier *Rule Britannia* (1972), Ch. 3, p.29

be reacting is typical of the book as a whole, and readers who disliked the novel, including Daphne's editors at Gollancz, found its wobbly tone disconcerting. The whole set-up of the plot seems farcical, but the way it is told – especially through Mad's cynical outspokenness – has a sharper satirical edge. By the end of Chapter 9, a corporal has been killed by 'one of the lethal arrows between his eyes' (p.119), and the comedy is looking black indeed.

But J.M. Barrie's enchanting vision of Neverland also casts its spell over these curious opening scenes. By arming Andy with bow and arrows, Daphne puts us in mind of the scene in *Peter Pan* where the Lost Boys are tricked into shooting at the Darling children on their first approach to Neverland. Emma plays the role of sensible mothering Wendy to the six boys, while eighty-year-old Mad in her Robin Hood jerkin is not only a legendary outlaw ready to taunt authority but Peter himself, the Boy who refuses to grow up. Like Peter Pan, Mad blurs the line between fact and fiction: 'Her life nowadays,' thinks Emma, 'was so frequently an elaborate game of make-believe' (p.14). But her theatricality affords her the sway of an artist over the emotions of her audience, and gives her the licence of a court jester to speak the truth. As the plot unfolds, she certainly does a more convincing and morally admirable job than the politicians. Being 'Mad' and refusing to conform, Daphne may be suggesting, could be a better way of seeing the truth and influencing the course of events than being time-serving and conventionally sane.

The theatrical element of *Rule Britannia* can also be found in *The Parasites*, which tracks the adult experiences of three children from a theatrical family. You will find it particularly intriguing if you are interested in delving into the biographical side of Daphne's writing, since there are suggestive parallels with the du Mauriers. In a letter reprinted in full in Margaret Forster's biography, she herself admitted that the three main characters – none of them particularly likeable – were her 'three inner selves, … the three people I know myself to have been' (p.421). The book give us glimpses into their very different inner lives. In the following scene, the actress, Maria, is sharing her marital problems with her homely sister, Celia, and her musical brother, Niall; but the reader is more privileged than Celia and Niall, since we are given sharper insight into Maria's private thoughts.

What is Maria saying in extract 18? And what is she thinking? Does this character tell us anything important about Daphne du Maurier's attitude to life?

Since Maria is a professional actress, we might assume that her tendency to identify with the parts that she plays can be explained as one of the occupational hazards of a stage career. Because she met her future husband when she was acting the lead in *Mary Rose* , a late play by J.M. Barrie, she now believes that the failure of her marriage can be understood by the fact that they fell in love under the illusion that the 'real' Maria was the same as the heroine, Mary Rose. This was no intentional deception: Maria admits that she herself saw her suitor through Mary Rose's eyes – until, of course, the part wore off, to be succeeded by other, equally absorbing roles.

But I suggest that this theatrical theme has a wider reverberation that sends ripples through Daphne's life and work. For other evidence of this, take a look back at the scene of John and Jean meeting in the bar in *The Scapegoat*, which was quoted in Section 5 (p.47). As the two men gaze at themselves in the mirror, John remarks:

> *We might have been two actors studying our make-up as we glanced from the looking-glass back to one another.* (Ch. 2, p.11)

The backstage world of costumes and greasepaint was utterly familiar to Daphne from her childhood visits to her father's dressing room. She had an instinctive feel for the way in which actors assumed role after role for the benefit of their audiences, and indeed how a famous matinée idol like Gerald had an image to maintain off-stage as well as on. This sense of an ingrained theatricality affected her view of human behaviour: for Daphne, the world's a stage, and all the men and women merely players. We take our different parts in one social setting after another, and act our way through life.

Fiction, like drama, is a way of exploring not a single authentic self, but the multiple identities we all have within us. I have put forward a similar argument in the section on the 'The man in the mirror'. Some parts we play out; other parts are merely potential, the selves we might have been. Play-acting, then, turns out to be the most serious, the most philosophical theme in Daphne's writing. No wonder she was offended when her readers persisted in thinking of her as a writer of superficial romances.

18. Maria shook her head.

'He doesn't really love me,' she said: 'he only loves the idea he once had of me. He tries to keep it in front of him always, like the memory of a dead person. I do the same with him. When he fell in love with me I was playing in that revival of *Mary Rose*. I've forgotten how long it ran – two or three months, wasn't it? – but all the time I thought of him as Simon. He was Simon to me; and when we became engaged I went on being Mary Rose. I looked at him with her eyes, and with her understanding, and he thought it was the real me, and that's why he loved me, and why we married. The whole thing was an illusion.'

And even now, she thought, gazing into the fire, as I say these things to Niall and Celia, who understand, I'm still acting. I'm looking at myself, I'm seeing a person called Maria lying on a sofa and losing the love of her husband, and I'm sad for that poor, lonely soul, I want to weep for her; but me, the real me, is making faces in the corner.

Daphne du Maurier *The Parasites* (1949), Ch. 3, pp.23–24

Writers and actors, therefore, have a huge and impossible job to do. They must lose their own identities in order to imagine other people's lives, and even when they are playing themselves, they have to hold something back. They need at all costs to protect that slightly detached, critical faculty that allows them to observe others, and themselves, in action, so that they can recreate situations on the page and on the stage. Like Maria, even in their most intimate confessional moments, they are 'still acting', watching themselves be sincere, while 'me, the real me, is making faces in the corner.'

If writers are obliged to commit themselves to one version of events, they are no more able to function than actors. At the end of *Rule Britannia*, in the last pages of fiction that she ever published, Daphne portrays the infuriating actress, Mad, close to death, flaunting her artistic licence to tells lies, her refusal to close off different paths to the truth. Mad is happy to call herself a 'mountebank': 'Rogues, vagabonds, strolling players,' she says, 'we're all alike' (p.307).

Mad's words express Daphne's defiant sense of her own art. Her books in all their variety and contradictions have to speak for themselves; they cannot be boiled down into a few formulae. Mad's words can also, perhaps, tell us something about her creator as a person. Daphne encompassed as many conflicting selves as any of the characters in her novels, expressing those various strands through her fiction. Maybe, then, we should look to her own imaginative writing rather than to the factual research of her biographers in order to understand her better. But we should be wary of thinking that we can pin down a single image of her. Is she Maria, Celia, or Niall? All of them, or none? Is she John or Jean? Male as well as female? Sane or mad ? She will always elude us – and while we are focusing on one of her public personae or fictional proxies, the real Daphne will be a little way off, mocking our efforts and making faces in the corner.

Ending Part One with *The Parasites*, a du Maurier novel that you may not have read, is a deliberate reminder of the scope of Daphne's work. Don't stick with *Rebecca* and other books you have heard of – her lesser known novels will reward your explorations!

PART 2

FIVE GREAT NOVELS

WARNING !

Plot revelations ahead – read the books before going on!

Choose one of these five novels, jotting down some ideas of your own as you read. Then look at the chapter.

These sections are designed to show the books from angles you may not have thought of. Your challenge is to decide whether you find these readings convincing, and to make a case in support of your own ideas.

Which interpretations put forward in the guide do you find most persuasive, and where do you strongly disagree?

Book Clubs

Consider assigning tasks to three members in advance of your meeting:

- quick plot summary of chosen novel
- personal response to main events, characters, themes
- summary of ideas in related chapter in the guide – to be debated at the meeting

1 *Jamaica Inn*
Of Merlyns and Men

One night Mary Yellan boldly leaves her bed in Jamaica Inn, and steals downstairs to eavesdrop on Joss Merlyn and the smugglers. Her uncle has sent her up after the gang's wild drinking session, threatening to crush her, body and mind, if she attempts any interference in the inn's lawless trade. But Mary has 'a demon of curiosity within her which would not be stilled' (p.53) and the courage to resist intimidation. What she overhears, as she listens at the half-open door of the bar room, is the gang threatening a man who wants to break with them – and what she sees, when all is at last quiet again and she judges it safe to move from her hiding place, is a rope dangling from a hook in the moonlight.

Daphne du Maurier is skilfully ratcheting up the suspense as her plot gets under way. Up to this point in Chapter 4, the reader has been unsure whether Mary's nervous fears about Jamaica Inn are well founded or primarily the product of a young woman's overheated imagination. Despite the story's impressive Gothic opening, which we examined in Part 1, there has been as yet little evidence to go on, and when Mary imagines on her first night at the inn that she sees a dead man hanging on a gibbet, it turns out that what she is looking at is only a creaking inn sign. The empty rope swinging from the beam is a more horrifying image, taken with the angry words that have gone before, and the reader is now pretty certain that an execution has taken place. But still, no evidence of murder is found. When a local magistrate breaks down the door of the locked chamber next to Mary's bedroom, two chapters later, in the expectation of finding a store of illegal goods, the only significant object in the empty room is a 'length of twisted rope' lying on a pile of sacks (p.85). Again, nothing is proven, but the sight of that rope has the power to generate a shudder in Mary and the reader.

Joss Merlyn's other criminal activities are subjected to more intense scrutiny – a kind of metaphorical tightening of the noose – as the plot races ahead. At first, the likelihood seems to be that he is engaged in the time-honoured Cornish profession of smuggling, and Mary is simply being asked to turn her head to the wall while the gentlemen go by. But Aunt Patience's excessive terror and the foulness of gang's behaviour suggest something much worse, which is unassailably confirmed in Chapter 8 in Joss's drunken confession of the atrocities he has perpetrated. The gang are ruthless wreckers – that is, not the retrievers of goods washed ashore from ships that have broken up, but cold-blooded murderers, setting false lights to lure ships onto the rocks.

Daphne is not drawing on local folklore here, but rather on upcountry legends about the wickedness of the western peninsula. There is no dispute about the terrible death toll among sailors on the inhospitable coast of north Cornwall, and you have only to visit the Victorian graveyard at Morwenstow, where Parson Hawker had to insist on his unsentimental parishioners burying the corpses and body parts washed ashore with the wreckage, to realise that shipwrecks were plentiful and even welcome events in the days of sail. But the representation of Cornwall as a land of savages, part of our national mythologising of the country's peripheries, was established in the eighteenth century in tales of West Barbary, and rooted more deeply in our culture over the next two hundred years. It is an image that Daphne was prepared to exploit shamelessly as a way of raising the stakes in her thrilling yarn of Jamaica Inn.

Joss Merlyn's drunken vision of the men and women he has drowned, which falls nearly midway in the book, is a set piece of tremendous melodramatic power. By concentrating graphically on the wretched victims, Daphne brilliantly recreates the horrors of the gang's brutal acts. But she also has a lurid fascination with man responsible for carrying them out, and the reader becomes mesmerised by the psyche of Joss himself. As Sarah Dunant points out, in her introduction to the Virago edition of *Jamaica Inn*, Daphne had been shocked by the nightmares that revisited her husband as a result of his experiences on the battlefield in the first world war, which gave her some personal knowledge of what it was like to share such mental distress. Joss's outpouring, the result of a potent brew of post-traumatic shock syndrome and delirium tremens, grabs the reader's attention and elicits – not a feeling of sympathy exactly – but a sense that we are witnessing a terrible tragedy in the suffering and fall of this giant-sized man.

Before the book is done, we get the action that we anticipate. Instead of listening to an account of a shipwreck, we find ourselves in Chapter 11

Jamaica Inn

18th-century coaching inn

Jamaica Inn, near the village of Altarnun on Bodmin Moor, was built in 1750 on the turnpike road between Bodmin and Launceston.

The idea for the novel came out of an eventful ride on Bodmin Moor in November 1930, when Daphne and Foy Quiller-Couch lost their bearings in the fog. They were staying at Jamaica Inn, then a temperance house, and their horses negotiated the bogs and delivered them back safely to the hotel. Daphne admitted that the popularity of her book was partly responsible for the dramatic changes that had taken place at the inn by the 1960s: 'Motor-coaches, cars, electric light, a bar ... As a motorist, I pass by with some embarrassment, feeling myself to blame.'

The inn is now a smugglers' theme pub, reached by a turning off the A30, with a room devoted to du Maurier memorabilia. The modern desk and the old typewriter came from Kilmarth; the old typewriter featured on a British postage stamp in a series on women writers in 1996.

Alfred Hitchcock's film

Hitchcock's version of Jamaica Inn *(1939) cast Maureen O'Hara as Mary and Leslie Banks as rough Joss Merlyn. The film was unconvincingly melodramatic, and made significant changes to the plot. Daphne hated it, complaining that her fearsome wreckers had been turned into* Peter Pan *pirates. Even worse, Hitchcock substituted a grossly lascivious squire (Charles Laughton) for the crucial figure of the evil vicar. The rescripting was necessary because of the Hays Code, which set out the moral guidelines for American film-making and specifically prohibited the portrayal of ministers of religion as villains.*

Maureen O'Hara as Mary – too beautiful and well spoken for the part – was given a more active role as heroine, cutting down a man who was hanged from a beam and warning off a ship which was heading for the rocks. Her sweetheart Jem was no Cornishman, but an incomer charged with bringing law and order to the district.

Jamaica Inn *was Hitchcock's last British picture. It gave little indication of the tremendous success that the director would make of his first Hollywood movie,* Rebecca, *released only a year later.*

actually on the shore, hearing the smash of a boat on the rocks and watching the wreckers get to work. But our angle on this scene is different from what we might have expected: rather than dwelling on the desperation of men drowning in the surf, our attention is focused on the savagery of the wreckers. Mary is scarcely able to stay conscious as the violence and destruction explode before her eyes. She herself is recovering from her struggle for personal survival, having narrowly escaped rape by the pedlar, the most disgusting of the gang. As the men fight viciously over the spoils from the wreck, and fall to murdering each other in their selfish panic to get away before daylight, we realise that we are being forced to witness the spectacle of men behaving like animals. Daphne du Maurier's ugly view of human nature, and of man's inhumanity to man, deserves closer examination if we want to get to grips with the underlying philosophy of *Jamaica Inn*.

Readers might have already caught hints of this important theme in the novel in some of its telling detail, not least the naming of the Merlyn brothers, who dominate the story. Merlins are wild birds of prey, entirely appropriate symbols for moor men like Joss, who hunt down their victims without mercy. But I want to argue here that the Merlyn name is only a small part of a much larger pattern, which is subtly influencing our attitude as we read. Even though we may be hardly aware of it, the novel is criss-crossed with references to animal behaviour. Some pick up on the wild life of the moors: the coach rumbles past the inn 'like a scared black-beetle'; the creaking inn sign is like 'an animal in pain'; and Jem's cart makes tracks 'like a hare' in the white frost. When the ship is drawn onto the rocks and turns on its side, it is compared to a sea creature, 'a great flat turtle'. People are repeatedly described as animals: Joss has the strength of a horse, the bulk of a gorilla, the teeth of a wolf. His wife shrinks from him like a kicked cur. The wrecking scene explicitly calls the men 'animals', as they squabble over the booty on the beach 'like monkeys'. Their leader, Joss Merlyn, lifts his 'great head' at the scent of dawn and sniffs the air like an untamed stag. Even Mary survives rape by her vicious counter-attack on the pedlar, causing him to squeal 'like a rabbit' before she flees from him 'like a hunted thing'. In this society, you hunt or are hunted. One particularly painful scene depicts the local idiot, tormented by the gang after a heavy drinking session at the inn, being stripped naked and chased into the night. Mary watches from the window, and sees *the outline of a quivering, naked form bound across the yard with great loping strides, screaming like a hare, and pursued by a handful of hooting, jeering men, with Joss Merlyn's giant figure in the lead cracking a horsewhip above his head.* (Ch. 4, pp.46–47)

Morality is absent from this Darwinian vision. This is a view of man as part of nature, and nature as red in tooth and claw.

The existence of the 'wretched half-wit', who mauls his ugly facial birthmark and squats on the floor of the inn 'like an animal', raises an even more uncomfortable question. Are some people more human than others? Mary is sickened by the cruel treatment meted out to this disabled man, but she is also sickened by the appearance and behaviour of the man himself. As she travelled across the moorland in the first chapter on her journey to Jamaica Inn, distressed by the contrast with the more civilised farmland community that she had left behind, she had sensed then that the moorland inhabitants might be a strange race which had adapted to its inhospitable terrain:

No human being could live in this wasted country, thought Mary, and remain like other people; the very children would be born twisted … Their minds would be twisted, too, their thoughts evil. (Ch. 1, p.13)

The novel is seriously concerned with the possibility that the development of people, just like lower animals, can be influenced by their environment, and that warped bodies might be a sign of warped minds.

These considerations come to the fore when Francis Davey, the Vicar of Altarnun, enters the story. The master-stroke in the plotting of the book is that Joss Merlyn is not the villain of *Jamaica Inn*. While we are coming to terms with the supposed leader of the wreckers – a man whose sheer bulk and magnetism, even in his gross moral and physical decline, give us an occasional glimpse of a man of tragic stature – the real villain has slipped past us in parson's dress. In the primitive fight for survival, a man of Davey's ruthless cunning has the advantage in the pecking order over Merlyn's brute strength. Davey deceives the reader as well as Mary, but it becomes apparent that if we had taken his appearance as an index of his nature, as Mary is inclined to do, we would have been on the right track. On her first meeting with the smoothly civilised vicar, Mary is instinctively wary because of his strange albino looks:

In the animal kingdom a freak was a thing of abhorrence, at once hunted and destroyed, or driven out into the wilderness. (Ch. 10, p.166)

Though she is half-ashamed of her uncharitable response, her logical thinking on the parallels between the human and animal world is of a piece with her overall philosophy of life. Since her gut instinct turns out to be right, the novel shows itself to be on the side of biology rather than morality. Francis Davey, as he is only too willing to admit, is 'a freak in nature' (p.274), an amoral creature who should have inhabited not only a pre-Christian but a pre-human era. In his satirical self-portrait, which Mary finds in a desk drawer at the vicarage, he depicts himself as a wolf preaching before a congregation of stupid sheep (pp.261–262). As he nears his end, he is compared to one of the most primitive life forms of all, 'a leech on the smooth surface of the rock' (p.291).

In the novel's penultimate chapter, where the evil vicar rides among the treacherous bogs and ancient crags of the pagan moors, he becomes, like the Merlyns, a bird of prey:

> *a hawk in the air, hovering an instant and brooding upon the grass beneath him, then swerving again and plunging to the hard ground.* (Ch. 17, p.281)

In the moment when he falls to his death, he seems to be transfigured into a bird, flinging out his arms 'as a bird throws his wings for flight' (p.292). He has been hunted down by a pack of hounds baying with an 'unearthly and inhuman' cry, and the man who has shot him is Jem Merlyn. The hunt is over, and as in the animal kingdom, Mary becomes the mate of the victor.

As Mary hesitates beside Jem's gypsy cart in the last lines of the novel, she faces south, her heart drawn to the tranquillity of her birthplace by the River Helford. Once she has made her decision and 'set her face towards the Tamar', she is not simply losing her loved home but ready to brave one of the worst trials that Daphne could devise: exile from Cornwall. Readers who may be unconvinced that roving Jem is a recipe for future happiness might take heart from the fact that Mary is an independent-minded woman, who is at least choosing heartache on her own terms. But why does she go, and why would most readers feel cheated if she had turned back?

Mary has tried to fight against her feelings for Jem, which are getting the better of her, 'when once she had been indifferent and strong' (p.159). She confesses: 'I don't want to love like a woman or feel like a woman ... ; there's pain that way, and suffering, and misery that can last a lifetime. I didn't bargain for this; I don't want it' (p.164). Mary is as clear-eyed in her understanding of the role of the sex instinct as she has shown herself to be about other animal aspects of human behaviour. She firmly believes that she has 'no illusions about romance. Falling in love was a pretty name for it, that was all' (p.137):

> *Men and women were like the animals on the farm at Helford, she supposed; there was a common law of attraction for all living things, some similarity of skin or touch, and they would go to one another.* (Ch. 9, p.136)

Village wooing would lead to traditional wedding, but inevitably, within a year:

> *the lad came home at evening tired from his work in the fields, and calling sharply that his supper was burnt, not fit for a dog, while the girl snapped back at him from the bedroom over-head, her figure sagging and her curls gone, pacing backward and forward with a bundle in her arms that mewed like a cat and would not sleep.* (Ch. 9, p.137)

Couples are domestic animals, no different from cat and dog, and their fate proves that romance is simply nature's way of ensuring reproduction.

Mary comes from more romantic stock: her mother had never taken a second husband because she 'belonged in body and mind to the man who had gone' (p.4). But look where writing 'a pack of giddy nonsense' (p.7) about her new lover, Joss Merlyn, had found her glamorous aunt only ten years later. The themes of violent men, vulnerable women, and miserable marriages run throughout the novel, and Mary sees clearly that her Aunt Patience has thrown away the chance of a happy home life 'to live like a slattern with a brute and a drunkard' (p.69). Jem admits that there is bad blood in the Merlyn family, which is particularly depressing news if you believe that heredity takes precedence over morality. He and his brother come from a line of womanisers and wife-beaters: 'I can remember my father beating my mother till she couldn't stand,' he tells her. 'She never left him, though, but stood by him all his life' (p.71). As Mary realises that her resistance to Jem's attractions is weakening, Joss and Jem, with their similar names, seem to her like Gothic doubles, two manifestations of the same man:

> *somewhere in the dark places of her mind an image fought for recognition and found its way into the light, having no mercy on her feelings; and it was the face of Jem Merlyn, the man she loved, grown evil and distorted, merging horribly and finally into that of his brother.* (Ch. 10, p.168)

Mary's fear is that Jem will become Joss, and that she will become her Aunt Patience. As the book ends, this could still be the eventual outcome.

'Why were women such fools, so short-sighted and unwise?' wonders Mary (p.69). And yet the Merlyn brothers exert a raw sex appeal to which she is only too susceptible. She has been prepared to protect herself against the risk of rape by her uncle since the night of her arrival at Jamaica Inn, but in a later moment of honesty she realises that 'aversion and attraction ran side by side' (p.140), and knows that her hatred for her uncle is intensified by her involuntary response to his maleness. The novel seems to endorse her preference for full-blooded men over more effeminate specimens: the Vicar of Altarnun has 'the voice of a woman' (p.161), which can be interpreted as a sign of his cold perversion. So, although she is fully aware that the magic at work is grounded in physical attraction – 'whether it was his hands or his skin or his smile' (p.137) – off Mary goes with Jem to Launceston fair on Christmas Eve, to sell Jem's stolen pony, buy a crimson shawl and golden ear-rings, and steal kisses in a dark doorway, for all the world like any country girl with stars in her eyes.

Under questioning, Mary might have defended her final capitulation to Jem in two ways. Sensibly, she could have elaborated on her belief that she had no choice: her animal instinct was too strong for her reason, and since Jem was her biological destiny, she had to make the best of her life with the mate who had captivated her. But, less sensibly perhaps, she might have continued to devise excuses for him. We have noticed earlier that she has been desperate to prove to herself that he was not, after all, a murderer or a wrecker, and it is true that he has shown no danger signs of meting out the kind of abuse that his mother and sister-in-law suffered. There is a reasonable chance, then, that he is not a Merlyn through and through, and that he might therefore shape up and treat his woman with some respect. After all, in the book's closing lines he does hand over the reins as soon as Mary joins him on the driver's seat.

And under similar questioning, I suspect that most readers hope that the plot will end with Mary's act of faith in Jem, and want to believe that this roguish hero will turn out to be a suitable husband – a rough Mr Rochester rather than a pitiless Heathcliff. In other words, we are dealing here with the myth of the redeemable man. Is it too cynical, in the light of all that has gone before in the novel, to suggest that the female reader's desire for a romantic ending is merely an example of her own animal will for survival at work? The whole project of romance writing, with its optimistic endings, may ultimately be part of nature's grand scheme to persuade women to put mating above more rational plans for our personal happiness!

2 *Rebecca*
The Serpent of Manderley

Rebecca's success as a pre-war bestseller was no surprise to its publisher, Victor Gollancz. It is an extraordinary novel with obvious popular appeal. From the evocation of Manderley on page one to the blaze on the horizon in the book's final lines, Daphne du Maurier's powerful plot holds the reader in thrall. There is no forgetting the haunting of Manderley by Maxim de Winter's dead wife, Rebecca; the agonising of Maxim's new bride; or the hatred of the spooky housekeeper, Mrs Danvers, towards the woman who dared to replace Rebecca. Engaging with the novel is a disturbing experience, as we are drawn into the tortuous thoughts of the nameless young narrator, the second Mrs de Winter, and find ourselves facing the primitive demon of sexual jealousy and haunting the border line between life and death. It was a strangely knowing book for a young woman of 30 to have written.

Every reader of the novel has a favourite scene. My mother, who identified with the shy narrator, would have remembered vulgar Mrs Van Hopper and Maxim's abrupt proposal of marriage to her young companion in Monte Carlo. And she would have imagined herself sitting in the car in that unfashionable stockinette dress on the newly-weds' return to Maxim's grand estate, as the second Mrs de Winter screws up her courage to face the household. For me, the most memorable tableau is the heart-stopping appearance of Maxim's new wife at the top of the staircase, when Mrs Danvers has tricked her into wearing the same outfit as Rebecca at Manderley's grand costume ball. Another shocking moment is marked by the explosion of the maroons in the fog, which bring Maxim's unhappy wife suddenly to her senses as she is on the point of falling from an upstairs window, urged on to her death by evil Mrs Danvers.

The rockets jolt the action forward, announcing the shipwreck that will lead to the discovery of Rebecca's boat on the bottom of the bay. *Je Reviens* is brought up with Rebecca's body still on board, and found to have been deliberately holed. The plot accelerates with Maxim's confession to his wife that he shot Rebecca out of jealous rage, when she hinted that she was carrying another man's child. But Maxim escapes a murder charge, after some intriguing detective work that supports the inquest verdict of suicide. Rebecca had kept secret the diagnosis of virulent cancer, her motive for taunting Maxim and courting death at his hands. But he is never free of his guilty knowledge that he has committed murder, and his Cornish neighbours have their own suspicions. As Maxim fully recognises, long before he sees the flames of Manderley lighting up the sky ahead, Rebecca has won.

There is a short period when Maxim's second wife refuses to accept Rebecca's dominance. She grows braver from the moment her husband tells her that he hated Rebecca, since he has put to rest her greatest fear: that her rival was not only more soignée and sophisticated, but more passionately beloved than she will ever be. In comparison with that dread, finding out that she is married to a murderer appears to pale into insignificance – if only Maxim can be protected:

> *'Rebecca is dead,' I said. 'That's what we've got to remember. Rebecca is dead. She can't speak, she can't bear witness. She can't harm you any more.'*
> (Ch. 20, p.316)

But she is wrong: Rebecca's triumph lies in her refusal to die. The raising of her boat from its watery grave should have freed the couple to begin a new life by bringing truth to the surface and putting an end to her power, but the name of her boat, *Je Reviens* (I Will Return), is a warning that she is a revenant. Though her body has been drowned and buried in the family crypt, her spirit is indestructible. She is capable of returning from the grave to inspire the burning down of Maxim's ancestral home, and she will live on to haunt Manderley even in their memories and dreams. The story told by Maxim's second bride, as the couple wander homeless around the hotels of Europe, is of a paradise lost.

For Manderley is Eden, and Rebecca its serpent. Daphne du Maurier's most famous novel retells one of the most potent myths of our culture, the biblical tale of the blissful garden that humanity can never regain. Manderley's lovely grounds encompass a Happy Valley, a paradise of fragrant white blossoms, but even here the pure beauty of nature has been tainted by the

The Garden of Eden – the Bible Story

Genesis, Chapter III

Now the serpent was more subtle than any beast of the field which the Lord God had made. And he said unto the woman, 'Hath God said, you shall not eat of every tree of the garden?'

And the woman said unto the serpent, 'We may eat of the fruit of the trees of the garden. But of the fruit of the tree which is in the midst of the garden, God hath said: "You shall not eat of it, neither shall you touch it, lest you die." '

And the serpent said unto the woman, 'You shall not surely die. For God doth know that in the day you eat thereof, then your eyes shall be opened, and you shall be as gods, knowing good and evil.'

And when the woman saw that the tree was good for food, and that it was pleasant to the eyes, and a tree to be desired to make one wise, she took of the fruit thereof, and did eat, and gave also unto her husband with her; and he did eat.

And the eyes of them both were opened, and they knew that they were naked; and they sewed fig leaves together, and made themselves aprons...

And the Lord God said unto the woman, 'What is this that thou hast done? ... I will greatly multiply thy sorrow ...; in sorrow thou shalt bring forth children; and thy desire shall be to thy husband, and he shall rule over thee ...'

So he drove out [Adam and Eve]; and he placed at the east of the garden of Eden, cherubims, and a flaming sword which turned every way, to keep the way of the tree of life.

In the next chapter of Genesis, Eve gives birth to two sons, Cain and Abel, and the first murder is committed when Cain kills his brother.

Alfred Hitchcock's Rebecca *(1940)*

Hitchcock's haunting black-and-white film – his first Hollywood picture – starred Laurence Olivier as the stiff Maxim de Winter, Joan Fontaine as his self-effacing second wife, and Judith Anderson as a brooding Mrs Danvers. Gladys Storey, a family friend of the du Mauriers, played Maxim's tweedy, no-nonsense sister, Beatrice. Rebecca *has been described as a 'Gothic woman's film', the first in a genre which (like the Gothic novels written by women 150 years earlier) created a psychologically threatening domestic atmosphere for a primarily female audience.*

There are important differences between the film and the book:

- *Hitchcock's Maxim does not murder Rebecca, who dies accidentally in a fall, and he therefore more readily keeps the viewer's sympathy.*

- *The film hardly begins to suggest the troubled mental state of the second Mrs de Winter, making her more wronged and pitiable (as well as more beautiful) than the narrator of the novel.*

- *Mrs Danvers is shown torching Manderley; in the book, we only guess that she must be responsible. She lingers with her candle beside the sleeping figure of the second Mrs de Winter in an unmistakable reference to* Jane Eyre, *and stands triumphant at Rebecca's bedroom window, dramatically silhouetted as the west wing collapses in flames.*

Despite the script's divergences from the book, Hitchcock's film is a powerful rendering of du Maurier's Gothic vision.

One effective scene, which does not feature in the novel, captures du Maurier's preoccupation with the intangibility of relationships and the instability of feelings. With a sly reference to his own black-and-white medium, Hitchcock shows the newly married couple at Manderley watching a ciné film of their happy honeymoon. But these bright moments are already in the past, as transient as their flickering presence on the screen. The projector stops when the domestic show is interrupted, brilliantly making Hitchcock's point that the joyful couple we have been watching no longer exist. Maxim and his wife at this point are beginning to fret that their hasty marriage will not bring happiness – an anxiety entirely in keeping with du Maurier's pessimistic view of romantic relationships.

presence of her predecessor, and the narrator finds the scent of the azaleas crushed white petals on Rebecca's boldly monogrammed handkerchief (p.133). In the Book of Genesis, when Adam and Eve have been tempted by the serpent to eat the forbidden fruit of the Tree of Knowledge, they are cast out into a fallen world where humankind's primitive instincts of sex and violence are unleashed, and the man and woman created for an eternity of joy are subject to the natural laws of reproduction, pain and death.

All this is foreshadowed, if we look for it, in the first chapter of *Rebecca*. Like Adam and Eve, the narrator in her dream yearns to return to Eden, but she 'could not enter, for the way was barred.' Once she imagines being spirited through the padlocked iron gates, she realises that Manderley's untended garden has been taken over by rampant plants. It is no longer an ordered paradise but a nightmarish jungle, and the language used to describe it is imbued with lust and disgust. You may find this hard to believe – you may even be shocked by the suggestion, especially if you have Hitchcock's film version in mind and recall the abridged words spoken by the lovely Joan Fontaine. But if you return to those famous opening pages and immerse yourself in du Maurier's prose, you will see how the guilty dreamer cannot disguise her hidden knowledge. (See the extract and commentary overleaf.) Her romantic memories of Manderley, though persisting, have been infiltrated in her mind by baser fears and desires. She has lost the innocence that Maxim so prized in her, and in that respect you could say that she has become Rebecca.

The Garden has known death before the second bride's arrival – there can be no doubt about that. Death is waiting to greet the second Mrs de Winter as she arrives at the great house in the form of Mrs Danvers, 'tall and gaunt, dressed in deep black.' Her face is 'parchment-white, set on a skeleton's frame', with 'great, hollow eyes'; her corpse-like hand is 'limp and heavy, deathly cold', 'like a lifeless thing' (p.74). We may recall the skull that is placed in old paintings as a memento mori, a reminder of our mortality. Wherever the new bride walks in the house, she risks an unexpected meeting with this 'black figure', whose eyes watch her from 'the white skull's face' (p.79). It is the housekeeper who brings the bride to the upper window in Rebecca's bedroom, hypnotically drawing her towards a suicidal fall (p.277). When Rebecca makes her secret appointment with death, to receive the London doctor's confirmation of her fatal illness, she aptly assumes the name of Mrs Danvers.

So who is to blame for bringing death into the world? And for sex and violence? According to the tradition handed down by the church, which runs deep in our culture, it is of course Woman. Since Eve was the one who

LAST NIGHT I DREAMT . . .

From Rebecca, Chapter One

Last night I dreamt I went to Manderley again. It seemed to me I stood by the iron gate leading to the drive, and for a while I could not enter, for the way was barred to me. There was a padlock and a chain upon the gate ... Then, like all dreamers, I was possessed of a sudden with supernatural powers and passed like a spirit through the barrier before me. The drive wound away in front of me, twisting and turning as it had always done, but as I advanced I was aware that a change had come upon it ... Nature had come into her own again ... The beeches with white, naked limbs leant close to one another, their branches intermingled in a strange embrace ... And there were other trees as well, trees that I did not recognize, squat oaks and tortured elms that straggled cheek by jowl with the beeches, and had thrust themselves out of the quiet earth, along with monster shrubs and plants, none of which I remembered. The drive was a ribbon now ..., choked with grass and moss ...; the gnarled roots looked like skeleton claws. Scattered here and again amongst this jungle growth I would recognize shrubs that had been landmarks in our time, things of culture and grace, hydrangeas whose blue heads had been famous. No hand had checked their progress, and they had gone native now, rearing to monster height without a bloom, black and ugly as the nameless parasites that grew beside them ... The rhododendrons stood fifty feet high, twisted and entwined with bracken, and they had entered into alien marriage with a host of nameless shrubs, poor, bastard things ... There was another plant too, some half-breed from the woods ...

The dream sequence at the beginning of *Rebecca* hints of Manderley's elegant past, a time when the blue hydrangeas in the extensive grounds were 'things of culture and grace.' When the dreamer eventually reaches the end of the overgrown drive, a page further on from the extract quoted opposite, she depicts the house lying in the moonlight like a beautiful jewel (a passage discussed in Part 1, pp.40–41). But the culture represented by Maxim's historic mansion has succumbed to the forces of nature, and now that the de Winters have been banished, 'Nature had come into her own again.'

The burgeoning growth obstructing the dreamer as she follows the drive with difficulty is not cool, restrained English greenery, but almost tropical luxuriance. On one level, this is not poetic licence but a realistic observation of the fate of such abandoned Cornish gardens, where Victorian enthusiasts once planted brilliantly coloured camellias and rhododendrons to take advantage of the warm, moist micro-climates in the southern valleys. The Lost Gardens of Heligan, which lie on the opposite side of the same bay to the Manderley estate (Menabilly), boast their own nineteenth-century tract of giant tree ferns, banana plants and bamboos, known as the Jungle.

But there is more than lushness in the dreamer's description. Hidden in her words lurks a fascinated revulsion to sexuality (*the white, naked limbs … intermingled in a strange embrace*), interwoven with a racialised language implying taboos of interbreeding with dark tribes (*jungle growth … gone native … monster height … black and ugly … alien marriage … half-breed from the woods*). Underlying the implied sexual content is the threat of violence in the verbs (*tortured … choked … twisted*), and down in the undergrowth lie contorted 'skeleton claws'. This is Eden after the Fall, an abandoned landscape of degeneration and death.

succumbed to the serpent's wiles and offered the apple to Adam, her punishment from God, according to Genesis, is to desire only her husband, who will rule over her. The snake must bear some share of the blame too, so the problem of who is most culpable is sometimes resolved in art by depicting the creature with the face of a woman. At Manderley, if Death is Mrs Danvers, the role of Eve-and-Serpent is played to the hilt by Rebecca.

Adam and Eve both eat the forbidden fruit, and know themselves to be naked. In other words, they discover their own sexuality and experience carnal desire. But again, the greater sinner is believed to be the woman. She is the seductress who creates lust in men and is therefore responsible for their desire to take revenge on women. Daphne du Maurier's Rebecca is the ultimate temptress, beautiful and vibrant, an anarchic femme fatale of unbridled sexual energy and flagrant immorality, luring men into her coils and inciting Maxim to murder. We learn that she had many lovers and indulged 'unnatural' bisexual leanings. Her louche cousin Jack Favell was at her beck and call. She attempted to seduce Maxim's bachelor agent, Frank Crawley, and his portly brother-in-law, Giles. Mrs Danvers, who adored her, claimed that Rebecca treated men as playthings and laughed at her conquests. Many readers will agree with Maxim that Rebecca's promiscuity has brought marital discord to Manderley – and may even accept that, when she is murdered, she is asking for it. Maxim's gunshot has a certain ring of justice, executing a woman for being a heartless, faithless wife and an unworthy vessel for the transmission of the de Winter line.

However, many readers have dared to admire Rebecca. Bold and dynamic, she was a fearless sailor, a dashing lover, and a consummate actress in her role as mistress of Manderley. She was an extraordinary woman, who defied convention to live her life to the full. A man would have got away with it – but a woman has to be punished. So she can therefore be understood as putting up a principled stand against the unfair biblical edict that her husband should rule over her and that her desire should be limited to his pleasure. Since the restrictions are designed to spare a married man the risk of being humiliated by a wrongful heir, Rebecca's promiscuity openly challenges men's hold over the inheritance of property. Maxim admits to avoiding a vulgar divorce for the sake of Manderley, his principal concern, but in doing so he lays himself open to the risk of a wife's sweetest revenge: giving birth to an heir that is not her husband's son. The plot seems to take his side, punishing Rebecca with the fatal condition of cancer of the womb.

In fact, according to her doctor's report, Rebecca could not have had children because of a uterine malformation. This apparently superfluous piece of information shows that Rebecca was indisputably lying about the possibility of being pregnant, and thus exonerates Maxim from having killed an unborn child along with his wife. But rather than fulfilling a practical function in relation to the plot, the fact seems primarily to have symbolic value, proclaiming Rebecca to be a wild sexual creature who could never have been domesticated by child-bearing. In Sally Beauman's luminous prequel to du Maurier's work, *Rebecca's Tale*, the injustice of her position as a woman in a patriarchal society is clearly apparent. Daphne's novel may not ask so blatantly to be read in the same way, yet such a reading undoubtedly has potential – and none of the evidence on which Beaumont bases her clever plot runs contrary to the detail in *Rebecca.*

The second Mrs de Winter is frightened and fascinated by sexuality. She fears Rebecca's powers, believing them to have given her the kind of hold over her husband that she could never emulate. She also fears finding those urges of desire and destruction in herself. Yet the more that Maxim wants to hide carnal knowledge from his second wife in order to preserve her innocence, the more tempted she is to seek out the secrets that her husband has forbidden. In Chapter 14, while exploring the west wing of the house, Maxim's new bride slips into Rebecca's bedroom. Like Bluebeard, her husband has shut these rooms up, but instead of her transgression revealing the butchered corpses of previous spouses, she suddenly dreads that she has found a living wife:

> *A satin dressing-gown lay on a chair, and a pair of bedroom slippers beneath. For one desperate moment I thought that something had happened to my brain, that I was seeing back into Time, and looking upon the room as it used to be, before she died . . . In a minute Rebecca herself would come back into the room, sit down before the looking-glass at her dressing-table, humming a tune, reach for her comb and run it through her hair. If she sat there I should see her reflection in the glass and she would see me too, standing like this by the door.*
> (Ch. 14, pp.185–186; author's punctuation)

Instead, the narrator sits herself down at the dressing-table, and catches sight of her own face in the mirror: 'The reflection stared back at me, sallow and plain' (p.187).

As she draws Rebecca's unwashed nightdress out of its case on the bed, Mrs Danvers enters and insists on conducting her on a tour of Rebecca's wardrobe as if she were Rebecca's dresser and lover in one. Determined to hold Rebecca at Manderley, Danny seems to believe that her clothes can keep her there:

> *She looked beautiful in this velvet. Put it against your face. It's soft, isn't it? You can feel it, can't you? The scent is still fresh, isn't it? You could almost imagine she had only just taken it off* ... (Ch. 14, p.191)

The eroticism of her language, her sensitivity to smell and touch, is stifling. Danny evokes an image of Rebecca lying seductively in bed with 'her mass of dark hair', and forces the new bride's hands into her little slippers. 'Harder, Max, harder,' Rebecca would say, as Maxim brushed her hair at the dressing-table.

The narrator, like the reader, is mesmerised. How deeply the scene has sunk into the unconscious of the second Mrs de Winter emerges in a dream she has in the last pages of the book, which reveals beyond doubt her hidden fear and desire of becoming Rebecca.

When the married pair first arrived at their new home, the drive before them 'twisted and turned as a serpent' (p.71). The image is picked up in the account of their second homecoming at the end of the novel as they drive back to Cornwall through the night. Having met the doctor in London, they have the vital piece of evidence that explains Rebecca's determination to die. But again, circumstances that should free the couple for a happier future fail to deliver their promise, and instead Rebecca once more tightens her grip. Maxim's second wife has a nightmare of being possessed by serpent-like Rebecca, imagining herself at Manderley, sending out invitations in the morning room in Rebecca's distinctive handwriting. When she goes to the mirror – that favourite device of Gothic fiction for giving insight into the strange other self –

> *A face stared back at me that was not my own. It was very pale, very lovely, framed in a cloud of dark hair.* (Ch. 27, p.426)

This is exactly the intimate marital scene which Mrs Danvers put into her head on her visit to Rebecca's bedroom in Chapter 14, when she sat on Rebecca's stool, only now the exchange is complete. She is Rebecca, seated at the dressing-table with Maxim erotically brushing away at her dark hair. But in the way of nightmares, the familiar becomes weirdly unfamiliar:

> *He held her hair in his hands, and as he brushed it he wound it slowly into a thick rope. It twisted like a snake, and he took hold of it with both hands and smiled at Rebecca and put it round his neck. 'No,' I screamed, 'No, no.'*
> (Ch. 27, pp.426–427)

This uncanny moment seems to hold more meanings than we can quite capture, though we feel that somehow we understand it. As the dreamer gazes transfixed into the looking-glass, a man is standing behind her, both lover and murderer. It is easy to half-read this passage as if Maxim were winding the hair around Rebecca's neck ('smiled at Rebecca and put it round *her* neck'), a prelude to her slow strangling. Sex and death are palpably close. But he is in fact coiling the snake around his own neck, like a noose. The dreamer cries out, presumably remembering that the man in the driving seat beside her could yet be hanged for murder. There are, however, more complex reasons for his wife's scream.

The hair snaking around Maxim's neck in the dream insidiously suggests that the serpent still has him in her coils. Maxim seems to be colluding in this act, since he twists the rope himself. Maybe his gesture implies acceptance of a guilt which can never be shrugged off, a recognition that his life will be for ever blighted by wife-murder. Or worse for his second wife, at some deeper level he may be willing to acknowledge Rebecca's sexual power over him, however vehemently he may hate her. Whether her husband is still under his first wife's sway or not, the dreamer can never wholly obliterate her instinctive knowledge of Rebecca the seductress. In her future mode of Maxim's companion, considerately reading him the cricket scores and keeping his mind off Manderley, she will never be able to supplant her rival in this sexual role. In the contest between the two women, the seductive rose and the innocent lily, vengeful Rebecca has irrefutably won.

The novel's vision, then, is of mutual betrayal in the sexual bond between men and women, a betrayal which will go on for ever. Women will always be temptresses; men will always be murderers. The most innocent of women will secretly desire to be vamps, and the most respectable of men will secretly desire their transformation. In the primitive and never-ending fight for exclusive possession of a mate, jealous lovers will be eternally watchful, poised to strike against rivals. Whenever we dream of returning to Manderley again, the drive will be 'twisting and turning as it had always done', the serpent of sexuality lying in wait for us in the beautiful garden.

3 *The King's General* The Romance of the Red Fox

The King's General is a love story, but a most unusual one. I have met du Maurier fans who rate this historical romance above all the novels they have ever read, hooked not so much by the absorbing account of the Civil War as by the bitter-sweet liaison at the heart of the story. But readers' feelings may seem misplaced when you consider how little time the lovers spend together in the course of a long book. Honor Harris never agrees to marry her King's General even in later life, when the fortunes of war bring them together again, and many chapters are taken up with Richard Grenvile's campaign against Cromwell's armies rather than with their renewed relationship. While Richard is away fighting, Honor is obliged to spend much of the war at the Rashleighs' manor house at Menabilly, and their meetings are again suspended. With the defeat of Royalist cause, Richard is forced to live out the rest of his days in exile, and the story closes on the lovers' long separation before Honor's advancing death. A curious outline, then, for a book affectionately remembered for its love affair.

It all begins promisingly enough with courtship among the apple blossoms:

> *Once a week, and sometimes twice, [Richard] would ride over to Lanrest from Killigarth, and there, cradled in the apple-tree … he tutored me in love, and I responded … Those March and April afternoons, with the bees humming above our heads and the blackcap singing, and the grass in the orchard growing longer day by day, there seemed no end to them and no beginning.* (Ch. 4, p.38)

This is pure romance. Honor's position in those branches is wonderfully precarious, her apple tree proving as tempting to her as to Eve, but we have no fear that she will fall into danger. Apple trees are magical in ancient legend, and if we know the old poems of knights falling asleep beneath their branches and being stolen away by the fairies, we might feel a Celtic glow emanating from those poetic Cornish place names, Lanrest and Killigarth. As the birds and bees celebrate the coming of spring, the lovers' time together has that everlasting quality of 'no end ... and no beginning.' But Honor's delightful initiation, followed by her 'wild betrothal, startling and swift' (p.46), comes to a cruel end. Her future is shattered by a hunting accident caused by the malice of Richard's sister Gartred. Honor loses the use of her legs – and, we understand, her physical capacity for lovemaking – for the rest of her life. The wedding is cancelled, and only five chapters into the novel we receive this sharp warning:

> *It was thus, then, that I, Honor Harris of Lanrest, became a cripple ... If anyone therefore thinks that a cripple makes an indifferent heroine to a tale, now is the time to close these pages and desist from reading. For you will never see me wed to the man I love ...* (Ch. 5, p.51)

The cruel curtailment of Honor's romance is a bold stroke for a book with hundreds of pages yet to go, and a reader familiar with du Maurier's writing might well interpret it as yet another instance of her stern lesson that lovers never live happily ever after.

And yet ... I intend to make the case that *The King's General* puts up a serious challenge to the cynical view of love which predominates in du Maurier's work. Daphne pulls off this uncharacteristic coup by overturning many of the premises of conventional romantic fiction. She devises a plot in which the lovers are kept apart, and moves away from springtime romance to midlife love. She refuses to treat her irascible hero as a redeemable man, letting him grow more brutal and boorish with the passing years. And she creates a spirited heroine as independent as the King's General himself by the extraordinary ruse of condemning her to a lifetime of disability. Despite all these departures from the rules of romance, the emotional tie between Honor Harris and Richard Grenvile seems very real to us as the novel draws to its end.

Nevertheless, the love story alone, intermittent as it must be, is not sufficient to sustain an entire novel, and the long periods of Richard and Honor's separation require other sub-plots to hold our attention. The lustful intrigues and lethal rivalries of Richard's sister Gartred provide several highly coloured strands. But the most striking pattern is woven around the hiding-place which opens into the room next to Honor's bedchamber at Menabilly. Here Honor saves Richard's terrified son from Parliamentarian soldiers scouring the estate for Royalist Grenviles, and Richard saves himself by crawling through the collapsed smuggling tunnel which leads from the cell to the sea.

As Daphne explains in her postscript to the novel, there really was a secret room uncovered in the buttress at Menabilly during building work in the early nineteenth century. Even more exciting for historians of seventeenth-century Cornwall was the discovery of a skeleton, identifiable by the surviving clothes and artefacts as a Royalist who had been protected by the Rashleigh family from Roundhead troops. When she took her lease on the house during the war, Daphne inherited the legend, the mainspring for *The King's General*, but despite hard searching she never found any positive proof of the chamber's existence. However, her biographer Judith Cook adds an intriguing coda to the story, confirming that she had personally seen the site of the cell, which had been exposed during further alterations to the house in 1980.

There is enough rich historical material in *The King's General* to keep readers involved in the unrolling story of the Civil War. Daphne had built up an accurate picture of the conflict from a Cornish angle through careful research. She was in touch with the Oxford don Mary Coate, who wrote the definitive history of the Civil War in Cornwall; she also talked with local historians, and the formidable scholar A.L. Rowse, who lived in the neighbourhood. There is no evidence to suggest that the seventeenth-century woman named Honor Harris, whose plaque is displayed in the nearby church at Tywardreath, was disabled, or that she was ever the mistress of Richard Grenvile. But Daphne's portrait of Grenvile – the Red Fox, as he was called by his enemies – conforms closely to Mary Coate's description:

> *he had a cruel and malicious temper, a mocking tongue, and an entire want of chivalry to a defeated opponent.* (Coate, p.131)

Recent research has further endorsed du Maurier's depiction of 'the King's General in the West'. The historian Mark Stoyle has strengthened Richard's claim to be considered a charismatic Cornish hero, who played the nationalist

Cornwall in the Civil War

Daphne's narrative of the Civil War is extremely accurate, though she adds fiction to the facts. There was even a Royalist immured at Menabilly, but not Richard's son. Most of her material comes from Mary Coate's fascinating study, Cornwall in the Great Civil War (1933).

1642: On the outbreak of war between Charles I's Royalists and the Parliamentarians

– the majority of the Cornish gentry take the Royalist side (including the Rashleighs of Menabilly), though others, especially in the south east, support Parliament (such as Lord Robartes of Lanhydrock)

– strong popular support for the King leads to the creation of a Royalist 'Cornish Army'.

1643: The 'Cornish Army' is victorious across the south west, but its respected commander, Sir Bevil Grenvile of Stowe, is killed in battle. Bevil's younger brother, the professional soldier Sir Richard Grenvile, returns from fighting in Ireland to join the Parliamentarians.

1644: Richard defects to the Royalists. Parliament denounces 'skellum' (scoundrel) Grenvile as a traitor; the Royalist press praises the 'Red Fox'. Now 'the King's General in the West', Richard recruits an impressive army by appealing to Cornish patriotism.

The Lostwithiel Campaign

A Parliamentarian army under the Earl of Essex, encouraged by Lord Robartes, unwisely crosses the Tamar and temporarily takes Bodmin. Among the houses sacked by Parliamentarian troops, as they are driven towards Fowey, are the Rashleighs' country house at Menabilly and their town house in Fowey. (Jonathan Rashleigh's accounts, detailing his losses, survive.)

The 'Cornish Mousetrap'

Royalist armies, led by Richard and Charles and strengthened by new Cornish recruits, successfully close in on Essex in the Lostwithiel area. Essex escapes by sea and his army surrenders to the King at Fowey. Cornish hostility is so fierce that only 1000 out of c.6000 Roundhead soldiers reach Devon alive.

1645: Richard leaves the siege of Plymouth to attack Taunton, where he is wounded. He pulls his men back into Cornwall. The Prince of Wales sets up court in Cornwall.

1646: Richard arrested for insubordinate behaviour and imprisoned on St Michael's Mount. Fairfax's New Model Army enters Cornwall. The Prince of Wales sails from Falmouth. Richard escapes abroad.

Hopton's Royalist army surrenders to Fairfax at Tresillian Bridge, near Truro. Sir John Arundell ('Jack for the King'), the Governor of Pendennis Castle, is finally forced to surrender. The Civil War in Cornwall is over.

1648: During the Second Civil War, rebellions in Cornwall at Penzance and on the Lizard are led by Cornish Royalists, including officers who served with Richard Grenvile. There is no evidence that Richard returns to join the rebellion.

1659: Death of Sir Richard Grenvile in exile at Ghent.

1660: Restoration of Charles II.

card to recruit and inspire his personal army. And with regard to Richard's temperament, Stoyle's discoveries have unfortunately confirmed that the King's General was, if anything, even more rude and ruthless than in Daphne's unflattering account.

The period that Honor spends at Richard's side during the campaign – eighteen months at Launceston and in various houses in Devon – takes up a long middle stretch of the novel. Since the book is written in the first person, it is essential for Daphne to find ways of keeping Honor close to the battle field in order to vitalise the events of the Civil War. Inevitably, perhaps, some of these devices seem artificial, and certain episodes lack the vividness of the scenes at Menabilly. Since the novel is backing the losing side, the later stages of the conflict also prove difficult to sustain dramatically. As the New Model Army marches closer to Cornwall under Fairfax's command, the reader may well be aware of the eventual outcome. We are removed even further from the action when Richard is arrested before the final stages of the war. His imprisonment on St Michael's Mount is a historical fact, though Honor is not of course in a position to give a first-hand account. Instead, Daphne embellishes the plot with Honor's undignified intervention in a highly improbable scene where she wins an audience with the Prince of Wales. Once the King's General has escaped into exile, du Maurier loyally reports the Royalists' brave stand and proud surrender at Pendennis Castle. She then turns an actual local rebellion into an invented opportunity to bring Richard back to Cornwall for the last time.

Cornish readers will be particularly grateful for the completion of the novel's account of the Civil War from the perspective of the far south-west. But the real strength of the book lies elsewhere, in giving so much of the conflict from Honor's viewpoint. Hers is the customary role of women, who have to endure separation and uncertainty while the men are away fighting. For Daphne, moving into Menabilly with three small children during the war years – even on one occasion being wrongly informed that her husband had been captured after the defeat at Arnhem – the contrast between the situation of men and women in wartime must have seemed stark enough.

Disabled and dependent on others for her protection, Honor also epitomises the powerlessness of all non-combatants left to fend for themselves in a war zone. Though occasional acts of resistance demanding a steady nerve and sense of purpose may arise, as in hiding soldiers from the enemy, most days go by in monotonous passivity. When Parliamentary troops plunder Menabilly, all that the rightful residents can do is eke out their rations and endure the pillaging of their estate. The book is especially convincing on the vicissitudes of conflict, and how it feels to live through a long-drawn-out sequence of hopes and defeats. One domestic vignette before Fairfax's final advance into Cornwall, in Chapter 25, strikes an especially poignant note.

Honor has returned to Menabilly for the hard winter of 1644/45, when the fearful residents are haunted by the spectre of the damaged house being occupied and sacked by the Roundheads for a second time. Richard joins the assembled families, and for a few January days there is a brief respite from hardship and separation. The men shoot duck in the snowy fields, the women watch, the children play, the lapwings wheel in the sky, and the sun comes out to dazzle them all. 'This,' thinks Honor, 'is an interlude, lasting a single second. I have my Richard ... Nothing can touch us for today. There is no war. The enemy are not in Devon, waiting for the word to march' (p.253). Daphne catches the moment perfectly, a fulcrum between the tribulations of past and future. But the families' few snatched hours of happiness are brought to an unharmonious end before the day is over, and the blame for breaking the spell falls not on the Roundheads but on the Red Fox.

Richard habitually spoils things by his selfish thoughtlessness, and appears to take perverse delight in doing so. As the couples gather round the fire on that snowy evening, one of the men deepens the nostalgic mood by crooning a love song. But Richard, insensitive as ever to others' feelings, ignores Honor's tender whisper, strums loudly on the lute, and sings an indelicate ditty. The party breaks up with the war once again pressing on everyone's minds, and 'all the quiet had vanished from the evening' (p.256). These few precious hours that Honor had hoped to treasure will hardly afford her the most romantic of memories. And sadly, this episode is not untypical of her brief encounters with her rough soldier-lover.

In company, Honor witnesses Richard's caustic arrogance and bad manners to others; in private, she has to bear his deliberate baiting and casual crassness. He mentions one day that his son Jo was sired on a country girl at the same time that he was riding over from Lanrest to Killigarth to make love to eighteen-year-old Honor in the apple tree, thus souring the sweetest memory of all. Known to be Richard's mistress, she suffers in his absence from damage to her own reputation, and from news of his indefensible brutality and mistakes on the field. However much he cares about her, Honor understands that love-making will always come a poor second to soldiering and furthering his selfish interests. Richard will never be faithful, and will sometimes simply forget her. He is, beyond question, an unredeemable man.

But it is precisely because Daphne does not follow the romantic formula in domesticating this rude Rochester, and because the heroine herself is under no illusions about his transfiguration, that the love story is the more credible. Honor bites her sharp tongue, humouring his moods and parrying his cruel wit with calculated nonchalance. Though she can exert only minimal influence over his behaviour and his temper, she puts up with her crude, bragging, sardonic, reckless, and eventually disgraced Richard, even as he grows more bitter and impossible to please with age. And the exasperated reader cannot wish that she had sent him packing, because there is no self-deception in Honor's acceptance of Richard's blatant shortcomings. When she decides to let her lover back into her life, she does so with her eyes wide open. Du Maurier succeeds in the feat of making this strange relationship a matter of satisfaction rather than aggravation to the reader by giving Honor the psychology of a woman disabled in body but not in spirit. By 'crippling' Honor, she has empowered her. After her accident, Honor cool-headedly realises that she would utterly lose her independence by becoming Richard's wife, or even his constant companion. On her marriage, she would not only be confined to the sphere of any wife of gentry rank, but compound her loss of freedom with her disability. With no tautness in the silver thread between them, she would become an encumbrance, left in a house of Richard's choosing while he travelled, fought and womanised as he wished. But by keeping the other end of that thread firmly in her own hands, she retains the role of an active and equal partner.

When Richard re-enters her life after fifteen years apart, we could see Honor as simply succumbing to the attractions of a bold cavalier, a sexy suitor but an impossible spouse. Yet he is a man whose faults she knows as well as his dubious charms, and she is clear that she could send him away again. Having made her decision, she is fully aware that she has lost the equilibrium that has taken her years to attain, and must live with the consequences. Realistically, the novel dwells on the emotions engendered by their separations more than on their brief times together:

> *It was easy for him, no doubt, to hold me close for five minutes and have me in a turmoil with his love-making, and then ride away to Launceston, his mind aflame with other matters; but for me, left with my hair and gown in disarray,*

and no method of escape, and long hours stretching before me to think about it all, it was rather more disturbing. I had chosen the course, though – I had let him come back into my life, and I must put up with the fever he engendered in me which could never more be stilled. (Ch. 13, pp. 123–24)

'I had chosen the course, though': it is Honor's steadfast refusal to fall into self-pity, or plead with Richard for more time than he intends to give her, which holds our respect. And a plot which keeps the couple apart for so much of their lives intensifies their meetings.

This is a midlife love affair, conducted in the full knowledge of the narrowing choices of older men and women. Honor might have rejected Richard and lived more contentedly, but she would have lost the memories that make up her heartfelt record of those years. Given the age expectancy of the time, when many people died in their forties, both war-wounded Richard and chair-bound Honor would have known at the end of the conflict that they were likely to be nearing the end of their lives. The last bitter twists to their tale are Richard's exile, and Honor's realisation that she has been supplanted as his emotional anchor by his grown-up daughter. But then, the reader reflects, would it really have been better for Honor to become the companion and carer of a cantankerous old soldier? Instead, she retires with her brother to reflect on happier days amid the calm of the Cornish landscape.

We have already heard the muted note of peaceful resignation in the novel's opening pages, as Honor watches the ebbing of the tide. (This passage is discussed in the first section of Part 1, pp.20–22.) The mood is autumnal, in contrast to the spring beauty of Richard's wooing in the apple tree so many years earlier. Towards the end of the book, we hear a similar strain. During the two-year lull between the Parliamentary victory of 1646 and the flare-up of the Royalist rising in Cornwall, when Richard briefly returns, Honor develops the custom of sitting alone outdoors in her wheelchair on the edge of the ravaged estate of Menabilly:

The sea is very white and still, without a breath upon it, and only a single thread of wash upon the covered Cannis rock. The jackdaws fly homeward to their nests in the warren ... Dusk comes slowly to the Gribben hill, the woods turn black, and suddenly, with stealthy pad, a fox creeps from the trees in the thistle park, and stands watching me, his ears pricked ... Then his brush twitches and he is gone. [author's punctuation] (Ch. 28, p.287)

This is a tranquil, natural scene, though the momentary appearance of the fox – a wild creature, bold and unreliable – is unsettling. It reminds us, of course, of Richard, with his irregular arrivals and sudden departures. Two chapters later, the Red Fox returns in person to disturb Honor's quiet, but this time, when he leaves, he has gone for good. From now on, the falling dusk, like the falling tide, will be untroubled and Honor's memories will be able to surface without interruptions and without regrets. Because of the mental strength with which Daphne endows her disabled heroine, this strangely convincing romance lingers with the reader long after we have closed the book.

4 *The Flight of the Falcon*
Who killed Marta Zampini?

This intriguing novel, set amid the crowded piazzas and Catholic churches of a busy Italian town, has understandably been overlooked by readers who think of Daphne du Maurier as a Cornish writer. However, it is a book not to be missed. Coming from the same stable as Daphne's classic fiction, it plays out on a different stage the dark themes of murder and rivalry which we have encountered in other novels. As a university town simmers with rumours, an arts director with delusions of grandeur is planning to release mayhem on the streets by the re-enactment of a thrilling medieval spectacle. But the truly important mystery to be solved before the dramatic dénouement is the murder of his childhood nurse, Marta Zampini, an event which puts him back in touch with the younger brother he lost during the second world war.

The Flight of the Falcon opens mundanely enough with the arrival of a coach party at a hotel in Rome, escorted by the novel's Italian narrator, Armino Fabbio. Most readers, like the tourists in his charge, would instinctively warm to Armino, a pleasant single man of thirty. His stature is hardly that of a hero: he is unexceptional in appearance, and self-conscious in the company of women about being rather short. But he seems amiable enough, friendly towards his colleagues, conscientious in his courier duties, and sensitive to his clients' needs. However, he readily admits to himself that a life spent shepherding groups of strangers for Sunshine Tours leaves something to be desired, a view certainly shared by his creator.

Daphne had spent an enjoyable holiday with her son and his wife in the medieval town of Urbino, a trip that proved to be the inspiration for *The Flight of the Falcon*. Her disdain at the behaviour of fellow tourists surfaces in the book in the naïve appreciation which Amino's clients show towards the synthetic experiences served up to them:

'This is the real Rome,' breathed Mrs Hiram Bloom, seating herself at a cramped table in a side-street outside a taverna brightly lit with pseudo-lanterns for her innocent enjoyment. Six musicians, wearing breeches, stockings and Neapolitan caps, appeared with beribboned guitars as if by magic, and my little party swayed in sympathy to their rhythmic strains. (Ch. 3, p.26)

Though the author appears to be inviting us to share her sense of superiority, Armino himself, though shrewdly aware of the deceptions passed off on tourists, is less critical and more complex in his response:

There was something endearing in their innocence and pleasure. I felt almost sad that tomorrow, perhaps, they would all be in Naples, no longer in my care. A shepherd has his moments. (Ch. 3, p.26)

His thoughtful care of his flock earns the reader's respect.

Like so many du Maurier protagonists, Armino is approaching a turning-point in his life, aware of some 'inner demon' urging him to make a radical change. The following snatch of dialogue shows that, although he is prepared to react against his brother's accusation of being a mere souvenir-selling tout, he knows that the inauthentic tourist experience he promotes to make his living is at odds with his search for personal integrity:

'They pay well,' I protested in self-defence, 'and I meet all sorts of people. It's experience, I'm travelling all the time ...'
'Where to?' he asked.
I did not answer. Where to, indeed ... (Ch. 10, p.120; author's punctuation)

When Daphne takes Armino back to his birthplace, he becomes reabsorbed into his home town. For the author, this plot development requires an equally bold leap, demanding that she abandon the safe vantage point of a postcard-purchasing visitor and enter imaginatively into the experience of a native Italian.

Before the end of the first chapter, the dramatic break in Armino's life that he has been unconsciously waiting for arrives. When his clients point out an old woman slumped in the doorway of a church, his attention is caught by 'that bowed posture, the ample drapery spread, the arms folded, the head buried under the weight of shawls' (p.8), and his memory sweeps him back to childhood. The old woman reminds him of his nurse, Marta, who was more of

Film Noir

The exposure of Daphne's generation to the cinema made it inevitable that her imagination would be suffused by film. The stage world with which Daphne was so familiar overlapped with the world of screen, and her father, Gerald du Maurier, made film appearances towards the end of his career.

Elements of her work are reminiscent of those black-and-white Hollywood movies of the 1940s and 1950s, inspired by crime fiction, which became known as 'film noir'. The Maltese Falcon *(1941), starring Humphrey Bogart, is arguably the first of the genre, but Hitchcock's* Rebecca *(1940) displays some of film noir's Gothic qualities. There are moments in the novel* The Flight of the Falcon, *as Armino pursues his investigations in the Italian streets, which show the influence of those classic films.*

Features of film noir

- *urban settings, where paranoia lurks in shadowy streets*
- *detective heroes with moral integrity but murky psyches*
- *desirable and menacing femmes fatales*
- *murder, passion, guilt, deception, and the elusiveness of truth*

Famous examples

The Big Sleep *(1946) – Humphrey Bogart plays Raymond Chandler's private eye, Philip Marlowe. Even tough Bogart gets a withering putdown from a woman for his less than heroic physique: "You're not very tall, are you?" – a disadvantage he shares with Armino in* The Flight of the Falcon. *But Marlowe and Armino have more important traits in common: genuine compassion and a commitment to seeking out the truth.*

The Third Man *(1949) – the best-known British film in this genre. Set in the streets and sewers of post-war Vienna,* The Third Man *evokes a corrupt city where an ordinary person bravely turns detective to solve the mystery of Harry Lime's death. Directed by Daphne's old flame Carol Reed, it gave a role to her sister Jeanne's little dog, which sat on the arm of the sinister 'Baron' Kurtz. The production company was British, but the co-producer was Hollywood's David O. Selznick, who had made Hitchcock's* Rebecca. *The screenplay was by Graham Greene, another influence on Daphne.*

a mother to him than his real seductress of a mother. Late that evening, after one of his male clients, a lone homosexual American, tips him a ten thousand lire note with an invitation to join him for a nightcap, Armino on impulse walks across the street and places the money in the hand of the sleeping woman. She may have opened her eyes and spoken his childhood nickname, Beo, but he turns away in denial, only to spend the night dreaming of being called. The woman is murdered overnight, and the two tourists who told him of the vagrant – a pair of bossy English women, unsympathetically coded as lesbians – insist on testifying to the Italian police. Armino takes this opportunity to look at the body in the mortuary, and finds himself gazing on Marta's face. Childhood memories flood back, and he abandons the tour to return to his birthplace and revisit his past.

Here we appear to have the elements of a murder mystery, with Armino cast in the role of private eye, investigating both Marta's past and his own. Armino himself admits to feeling 'like a detective out of a police novel' (p.48) as he follows a man who once knew Marta through the narrow streets of Ruffano. At certain moments we seem to be immersed in a black-and-white film of the 1940s; when Armino, having left the mortuary in Rome, tells us: 'I turned up my coat collar, pulled my hat low and threaded my way through side streets to the via del Tritone' (p.24), cinema lovers may glimpse a Bogart-like figure slouching in the shadows.

Like many private investigators in crime movies, Armino is a quiet man with a troubled inner life. Marta, he feels sure, was murdered for the money he gave her, but he fears that telling the police will raise suspicions that he is the killer. He begins to feel more villain than detective, coming to believe that the police are tracking him down. However his return to Ruffano gives another twist to the plot, sidelining Marta's murder for much of the novel. Beo discovers the shocking truth that his older brother, Aldo Donati, believed to have been shot down during the war, is not only alive but holding the prestigious post of Director of Arts in Ruffano. Aldo in his turn has accepted that Beo must be dead. The real mystery to be unravelled is about the original family on which two grown-up men have built their separate lives.

As a boy, Aldo dominated the little brother who adored him by force of personality, and the frisson of fraternal sadism evident in their childhood power games has its reverberations in adulthood. Beo remembers being repeatedly shut in the linen closet to re-enact the nightmarish scene of the raising of Lazarus, depicted in a horrifying altar-piece in their local church. Beo was forced to wait in the closet for the terrible moment when he was called out of the tomb to face Aldo, not knowing whether his brother would be waiting in the garb of a loving Christ or a black Devil. Good Brother or Bad Brother? Beo is never sure, but remains Aldo's devoted disciple. On his return to Ruffano, he has at last one small advantage over his brother. Since he is utterly unexpected, unrecognisable, and living under a different name (having taken the surname Fabbio from his stepfather), he can at last choose his own moment to walk out of the linen closet and reveal himself.

Aldo, as dangerously charismatic as ever, is master-minding an ambitious festival, planned around the historical re-enactment of an event that took place five hundred years ago, when the corrupt Duke of Ruffano, known as the Falcon, drove a chariot with eighteen galloping horses through the streets to the ducal palace. While men fought each other in the chariot's wake, the megalomaniac Falcon donned Icarus-style wings and leapt from a turret to his death. Aldo is acting out his mirror roles of Christ and Devil on a grand scale, inspiring his followers with inflammatory speeches and inciting violence between the students of rival university departments. At the core of his entourage is a band of twelve disciples who carry out his bidding, carefully picked for their vulnerability as children orphaned or mistreated in childhood. Here we find yet another reincarnation of J.M. Barrie's Lost Boys, and the suicide in 1960 of Daphne's cousin Peter – one of the brothers for whom Barrie created *Peter Pan* – may have been one of the hidden factors in determining the culmination of this bizarre plot. Beo is inevitably co-opted into Aldo's dramatic spectacle, and survives a symbolic trial of his courage when he joins his brother in the dangerous chariot drive to the palace. He plays his own part successfully to the end, but he is powerless to prevent Aldo's fatal restaging of the ultimate death-defying scene of the Falcon's life. This gives Beo the chance of a new future. Once Aldo is dead, he is ready at last to shed his assumed surname, and step up into his brother's place as the worthy public representative of the Donati family.

The crucial turning-point of the plot is the discovery that Aldo was never Beo's elder brother. He was an adopted child, a cuckoo in the family nest, born illegitimately to Marta Zampini, who agreed to enter the household as his nurse. Aldo's personal house of cards collapses when Marta tells him the truth, and as the sequence of revelations unfolds, Beo suspects his brother having gone to Rome to kill Marta. In the hysterical atmosphere of Ruffano, where crowds are caught up in Aldo's make-believe pageant, the reader becomes no more certain than Beo about the distinction between make-believe and reality. The real killer, however, turns out to be an anonymous thief, who finally confesses to the double crime of robbery and murder.

But since this is much more than a detective novel, the brothers are not exonerated by the official explanation. Marta would not have been a vagrant in Rome, had Aldo not rejected her in Ruffano and, as Aldo recognises, his crime goes deeper:

> *'Yes, I killed her,' he said, 'but not with a knife – the knife was merciful. I killed her by despising her, by being too proud to accept the fact I was her son. Wouldn't you say that counts as murder?'* (Ch. 23, p.299)

Beo has also had a hand in Marta's death, just as he feared. But it is not only by leaving that ten thousand lire note and turning away from her that he is implicated. His reply to Aldo acknowledges that he is no less blameworthy than his selfish brother in dishonouring the closest bond of all:

> *I thought … of my own mother who had died of cancer in Turin. When she had scribbled me a line from hospital, I had not answered.*
> *'Yes,' I said, 'it was murder. But we're both guilty, and for the same cause.'*
> (Ch. 23, p.299)

Armino, a gentle and courteous man towards other people, has lived his adult life idealising his memories of his motherly nurse Marta while condemning his birth mother. His 'beautiful slut of a mother' (p.29), as he calls her, died of cancer of the womb, a punishment for her unmaternal behaviour that both brothers seem to feel is deserved. (Rebecca, you may remember, was dealt the same fate for her defiant infidelities.) She self-indulgently trailed her child Beo along with her when she left Italy as the mistress of a German commandant. As the fortunes of war swung in favour of the Allies, she transferred her affections to an American brigadier, ending her life with an Italian husband. Marta, on the other hand, has a name that sounds as if it combines the self-sacrificing qualities of a 'martyr' with the homeliness of Martha in the New Testament. Or 'Marta' could simply be heard as 'mater', one way of pronouncing the Latin word for mother: therefore, a generic mother figure. This Bad Mother/Good Mother contrast is based on the age-old construction of women by men. Women can be only whores or angels, Mary Magdalen or Mary the Virgin Mother. The religious overtones are intensified by the setting of this novel in a Catholic country. But Armino is not allowed to get away with this simplistic male view, though it certainly colours his response to other women he encounters throughout the book. The maternal bond cannot be so easily shrugged off, and Beo realises that the act of disowning his 'beautiful slut of a mother' – or even thinking of her in those terms – is a sin in itself, as culpable as Aldo's rejection of his birth mother, or the pitiless killing of an abandoned old woman.

The sense of guilt that pervades the novel is enhanced by playing on our ideas of Italy, past and present. The ancient ducal palace, with its turrets and hidden spiral staircases, conjures up 'that sinister and unknown world of poison and rapine, of power and beauty, of luxury and filth' (p.200) which we associate with the medieval cities of the Borgias. Modern Ruffano is corrupt in a different way, a hothouse of salacious gossip and sexual licence. Armino's first encounter in the town is with the young lecturer Carla Raspa, a rapacious femme fatale, whose emergence for the evening in a stiff black skirt, her lips 'bloodless', prompts Armino's thought: 'A vampire, before swooping to feed upon its victim, could not have looked more dangerous' (p.169). Disgusted from childhood by the 'stench' of his mother's lust (p.237), he at least has some psychological excuse for his attitude, and his gentle nature prevents him from taking advantage of women. Meanwhile Aldo, self-centred by nature and unrestrained by his conscience, is conducting an affair with the University Rector's gracious wife at her own house, once the Donatis' family home. Bored with female adulation, he refuses to admit any difference between his sensitive Chopin-playing mistress and the brazen Carla Raspa, who flings herself at him: 'They both wanted one thing only. Carla Raspa happened to be more honest about it' (p.256). He has no compunction about stirring up factionalism within the University by manufacturing sexually sinister incidents: the respectable spinster in charge of the women students' hostel is subjected to a titillating mock rape, and a male head of faculty is humiliated by being stripped naked and tied down in public view, an incident that grows into a rumour of his emasculation. One of Aldo's victims is subjected to threats of torture by his masked henchmen in the palace, another sign of his resurfacing boyhood sadism. In his emulation of the Falcon Duke, he is treading very close to the boundary with barbarism.

But Aldo himself would insist that this confusion is hardly surprising in a country overshadowed by the recent war. As boys, he had worn the black shirt of Fascist Youth, while Beo had waved a swastika flag from the car of a German commandant. Now, though democracy has returned to Italy, everyone's lives have been unforgettably seared by the past. Aldo is never happier than when he can excite the extreme passions experienced in wartime.

He seems oblivious to his moral responsibilities as he toys with the risk of inciting mob violence, and his rabble-rousing rhetoric is uncomfortably reminiscent of the word power that made dictators of Mussolini and Hitler. However, he is not alone in bearing the psychological scars that the war inflicted. The horrors of death-camp torture and battle-field carnage are too close for anyone in Europe to feel innocent. As the German tourists shoot their ciné films, they move their cameras 'slowly from side to side like a machine-gunner sweeping his field of fire' (pp. 28–29). Everyone of their generation has memories from the time of conflict on their conscience.

War brings out the worst in people, but peacetime makes it harder to disguise our daily trespasses. It is part of Aldo's philosophy that we all have a 'motive for murder' at some time or other (p.125). Daphne agrees. We are back in the dark du Maurier world where we all have something, or someone, to feed our guilt, remembering how we rejected or took revenge on those closest to us. Thinking back to *Rebecca* and *My Cousin Rachel*, we can recall two typical endings that take us round to the start of the books in an endless loop of suffering and guilt. Maxim de Winter and his wife, who both wanted Rebecca dead, are banished from Manderley for ever; Philip Ashley can never know whether he was responsible for the death of an innocent woman, so he will always be haunted by the murderer's corpse, the image that opens and closes his narrative. There is no peace for the wicked in these classic du Maurier works.

The Flight of the Falcon, however, seems to offer a way of breaking that vicious circle. Aldo makes his own decision to fall free of his past, choosing to die in an existential moment of glorious self-assertion. But it is his unassuming little brother – decent, likeable, unambitious Beo – who manages to redeem himself. In this novel there may be, after all, some way of placating our inner demon and absolving ourselves. The narrator's integrity in attempting to clear up the mysteries of his own past has brought its reward. We end the book with guarded optimism, trusting that Armino will take his rightful place as head of the Donati family, and complete his personal circle by finding a fulfilling role for himself in the town of his birth.

5 *The House on the Strand* Trysting with Isolda

The writing of *The House on the Strand* marked Daphne's transition to her last home at Kilmarth in much the same way that *The King's General* had celebrated her arrival at Menabilly twenty-five years earlier. The touch paper for her Kilmarth novel was the discovery of laboratory bottles containing animal embryos left by a previous occupant in the rambling basement – not as romantic a find as the Royalist skeleton at Menabilly, but equally combustible once ignited by Daphne's imagination. Out of those objects she conceived the plot of a scientifically developed time potion which could transport the drinker to the medieval period of Kilmarth's foundations.

The novel supposes a link between the house's summer occupant, Dick Young, and the steward of the fourteenth-century estate, Roger Kylmerth, who had dwelt on the same site. At Roger's side the unseen modern traveller, having bridged the time gap, can watch events unfold at close quarters. How close is apparent from his first encounter with the steward, who is mounted on a sweating pony:

> *Both exhaled a pungency so strong that they seemed of the essence of life itself. The sweat-streaks on the pony's flanks, the shaggy mane, the fleck of froth at the bit's edge; and that broad knee in the stockinged leg, the leather jerkin ... this was reality, I the alien presence. I longed to stretch out my hand and lay it on the pony's flank ...* (Ch. 1, p.5)

The narrator's nearness to horse and rider is palpable, the senses over-excited. The sheer physicality of the relationship with these living creatures from the past – the smell, the froth, the man's knee and the pony's flank – create an even more 'in-your-face' reality than normal experience.

Although it is impossible for a man from the future to influence this past, and any attempt to make physical contact instantly breaks the connection, the modern observer is in danger of being drawn into the spectacle. He may be bodily detached but he cannot be protected from emotional immersion. This is the tragedy of Dick Young, a middle-aged Englishman, who has given up his publishing career in London to rethink his life. The plan is to spend a summer with his family – his new American wife Vita and her two sons – at a friend's second home in Cornwall. Kilmarth is owned by a former schoolmate and college crony, who has made his name as a professor of science. Always the suave senior partner in their vaguely homo-erotic relationship, Magnus becomes Dick's magus, urging him with a stream of letters and phone calls from his London laboratory to experiment with a new drug. Unsure about his own future, disillusioned with his work and depressed by the demands of his wife, Dick plunges into a more vibrant past, putting his health and his marriage at risk in pursuit of his Kilmarth predecessors, and of one beautiful woman, Isolda of Carminowe.

The House on the Strand was Daphne's penultimate novel, written at a time when she feared her creative powers to be on the wane – her personal anxieties, I will argue later, found their way into her conceptualisation of the story. In fact the book turned out to be as impressive as the work of her prime. She was, of course, writing about her home territory, and the map provided with the novel shows the sites she explored to the north of Kilmarth. She already knew how the landscape had changed over the centuries from her research into the seventeenth-century terrain of *The King's General* and the sixth-century locations associated with the legend of Tristan and Isolda, which she retold in *Vanishing Cornwall.* Her map sketches in the higher sea level in the days before the silting up of Par Bay, when it would have been possible for Otto Bodrugan's boat to navigate upriver as far as Treesmill. As a yachtswoman herself, she also understood the Cornish people's dependence on the sea as an essential means of travel. On many occasions, she had made the short voyage south across the bay to the headland at Chapel Point where Sir Otto's estate lay, landing for picnics on Colona Beach where Dick disembarks during his family fishing trip in Chapter 12. For the purposes of the novel she had carefully traced her narrator's steps up the valley to the farmhouse, still known as Bodrugan Barton, where Dick notes the barn that was once a medieval chapel (p.151).

Daphne's careful historical reconstruction in *The House on the Strand* is evident in the detail, right down to the inclusion of a family tree, but her

Tristan and Isolda

The myth

Tristan is sent to Ireland by his uncle, King Mark, to bring back the princess Iseult (Isolda) as his bride. However, a love potion administered on the journey causes Tristan and Iseult to fall passionately in love. Tristan later travels to Brittany and marries another Iseult (Iseult of the White Hands), but he returns to Cornwall and is murdered by King Mark. In another version of the ending, he sends for his Cornish Iseult as he lies wounded in Brittany, telling her to hoist white sails on her ship if she is on board. He is told that black sails are approaching, and dies before she reaches land.

The history

Castle Dor, near Fowey, may well have been the fortress of a 6th-century Cornish ruler named Mark. The 12th-century Norman poet Beroul, who visited Cornwall, gave the lovers Cornish names and located Mark at Lancien. The word has been identified with modern Lantyan, a farm close to Castle Dor. He also described a meeting of the lovers at Mal Pas, still the name of a crossing place on the River Fal near Truro.

In Vanishing Cornwall *(1967), Daphne described her searches around Castle Dor, convinced of the truth in the legend. She had recently moved into her last home at Kilmarth, and was delighted to find that the Cornish name translated as 'Retreat of Mark'.*

The Tristan Stone

One vital piece of archaeological evidence in support of the Tristan legend is an impressive pillar of stone on which are carved the words: DRVSTANVS HIC IACIT / CUNOMORI FILIVS *(Drustanus lies here, son of Cunomorus). Marcus Cunomorus was the 6th-century ruler known as King Mark, and his son Drustanus may be the legendary Tristan.*

The pillar stood for many years at Four Turnings, outside the lodge gates of Menabilly (on the very spot occupied by the dreamer at the opening of Rebecca *and the gallows at the beginning of* My Cousin Rachel*). Nowadays you will find a mini-roundabout there, and the Tristan Stone has been moved to the left-hand verge of the approach road to Fowey.*

Castle Dor

On the death of her friend Sir Arthur Quiller-Couch (Q), another Tristan enthusiast, Daphne agreed to complete his novel Castle Dor *(1962). The romance takes as its premise the curious influence of the past on the present, telling the story of a pair of 19th-century lovers who seem fated to retrace the ancient paths of Tristan and Isolda.*

scholarship put no brake on her fertile inventiveness. By chance she had happened on a wonderfully rich historical period in Cornwall, laced with evocative names. The local gentry really were called the Champernounes, the Bodrugans and the Carminowes, and Dick's beloved adulteress was actually named Isolda. The colourful rivalries and rebellions of the fourteenth century, ending in the terrible scourge of the Black Death, fuelled Daphne's growing excitement over the progress of her research and translated effectively into Dick and Magnus's sleuthing in the archives. In the episodes where the novel crosses into the past, her powerful imagination takes over and transforms these well digested facts into memorable fiction.

The medieval scenes that play before Dick's eyes are full of action and atmosphere. We see death beds, monastic decadence, children's games, the cruel interrogation of a young spy, the slaughter of farm animals for a feast, brutal murder, passion and plague. Dick never knows whether he will arrive in daylight or darkness, what the season will be, or what extremes of weather will greet him: a primrose-filled spring, a sailing ship tossed by autumnal storms, or an otter hunt in the snow? The call of the cuckoo has the resonance of medieval folksong, and the vivid pictures of a 'hooded musician with his double horn' and a woman with a jewelled fillet in her braided hair (p.50) have the quaintness of pictures in an illuminated manuscript. No wonder Dick is reluctant to return to his own day of rattling railway engines, littering tourists, unwanted guests and marital strains. As he struggles back to consciousness, the strident sound of the telephone ringing is 'like a summons from a lost, unwanted world ...' (p.11).

The modern landscape around Kilmarth in *The House on the Strand* has none of the romance we associate with 'du Maurier country'. While beaches and boat trips keep his family occupied with holiday Cornwall, Dick is drawn inland to the site of the Benedictine priory and to the manor of 'Tywardreath', which means literally 'the house on the strand'. As he stumbles around the railway tracks and old mine workings that scar the fields, searching for evidence of the ancient buildings that lie beneath, he is sometimes briefly in touch with the countryside of his own past, an idyllic domain of bird's-nesting and boyhood freedom. More often, however, he is frustrated by the ugly camper vans and bungalows that obstruct his desperate quest for the district's history. He returns to consciousness after one journey to find himself in an abandoned quarry with the débris of modern capitalism at his feet – old cans, a tyre, a broken bedstead. Yet when he returns to the medieval realm, the same dreary places are bathed in technicolour.

Roger Kylmerth's society lives more intensely, less bounded by control and convention than Dick's twentieth century. Its passions and rivalries erupt into action, while below the surface run undercurrents of treachery, adultery, ambition and violence. Much of the complex political and domestic narrative which Dick begins to unravel is grounded in a historically plausible reconstruction of events. Marriages were indeed arranged among gentry families of the south west in the interest of consolidating land and social influence, a coercive context that promised domestic disharmony on a grand scale. Dick was right to assume that women of high-ranking families became 'Goods reared for purchase, then bought and sold in the market-place, or rather manor' (p.34). But the Isolda sub-plot at the core – providing Dick with the love of his life and the vicarious opportunity to put himself in the role of a bold and glamorous suitor – is pure romance, and Daphne creates *Frenchman's Creek*-style episodes of Sir Otto Bodrugan sailing over the bay from Chapel Point and slipping into the creek at Treesmill for an assignation with his Isolda. But if *Frenchman's Creek* is light-hearted comedy, the tale of Otto and Isolda is tragedy – not Dona and her pirate, but Tristan and Isolda. Otto is ambushed and ruthlessly drowned by Isolda's husband and his men, and at this mid-point of the novel, things begin to go horribly wrong on both sides of the time divide. The dynamic of *The House on the Strand* depends on holding past and present in tension. Dick and Magnus move between two worlds, which collide disastrously when Magnus, under the influence of the drug, attempts to cross a railway line where the medieval river used to run, and receives a fatal head wound from a passing freight train. Dick suffers from worsening side effects as he returns addictively to the medieval scenes that haunt his waking life, beginning to fear that the two are starting to merge in his head. His confusion spirals out of control when Roger chivalrously rescues Isolda – having always loved her, without hope, as Dick has come to do – and brings her to sleep under his roof at Kilmarth. When her enemy, Joanna Champernoune, arrives with an entourage to threaten Isolda and take her away, Dick moves angrily across the centuries to intervene, waking to find his hands on his wife's throat. With unbearable irony, at the point when he has followed the medieval story to its end, taken the final dose of the drug, and feels free at last to move on with his future, Dick is overtaken by physical symptoms that may be the precursors of worsening paralysis.

Carried along by the momentum of the gripping plot, the reader is intermittently aware of a more intellectual strand in the book's weave about the nature of time travel. Daphne had to provide some explanation of Magnus's drug simply to make the story plausible, and her detailed changes to the typescript (which can be seen in the du Maurier archives in Exeter) show that she worked hard at finding appropriate scientific terms to describe the brain's response. But the theorising is taken further, as Daphne explores different avenues to explain the time phenomenon. Dick wonders about a 'fourth dimension' accessed through place, since Kilmarth seems to be the key to his connection with Roger. Magnus develops a more complex hypothesis about an inherited ancestral part of the brain, a theory that Daphne, with her interest in the ideas of Karl Jung, might herself have entertained.

The alternative, of course, is that Dick's experience is a hallucinogenic illusion. The local doctor who interests himself in Dick's case sees him as an impressionable addict in a particularly susceptible phase of his life, using the drug to create a kind of dream world that mirrors his own. Since Dick's marriage has become arid, he fantasises freely about the untouchable Isolda. It is therefore no accident that he meets a beautiful woman in his drug-induced trips into the past, whereas homosexual Magnus finds himself in the monks' dormitory. Isolda embodies the desirable woman he wishes Vita to be, Joanna Champernoune the hard bossy woman Vita has become. Isolda's two daughters can be interpreted as a straightforward transformation of Vita's two sons. The reader quickly catches on to the argument and pursues other implied parallels. Roger falling sick of the plague may thus be a sign of the malfunctioning of Dick's physical body. There is even a suggestion that Roger's death heralds the death of the man who has dreamt him up, since at some instinctive level of his psyche, Dick might know that he is doomed by irreversible chemical changes in his brain.

But for a midlife romantic like Dick, who is searching for significance in his time travelling, to reduce his experience to an account of his brain's behaviour is sacrilegious. He does not want to think of himself as a deluded fantasist, who can find a cure by weaning himself off the drug as his doctor proposes. Nor does he want to be one of Magnus's biological experiments, a kind of laboratory animal, whose trips into the past can be accounted for by observable brain patterns. When he decides to get rid of the contents of the Kilmarth cellar, so that they cannot be investigated by the police before Magnus's inquest, he destroys the bottled monkey's head with a particularly vindictive thoroughness:

> *I took one of the dead branches and scraped a pit in the wet, dank earth and emptied the sack into it, smashing the monkey's head with a jagged stone so that it no longer bore any resemblance to a living thing, only fragments, only jelly...*
> (Ch. 17, pp.223–224)

It is frightening for most of us to think of our minds as being no less corporeal and comprehensible than a monkey's, so that we can lose control when a problem arises in the wiring. At least Magnus's scientific approach allows for the possibility of an ancestral memory box, which gives some genuine access to the past; after all, he and Dick appear to have experienced the same place and period in ways which go beyond mere chance or mutual suggestiveness, and the people they meet are historically verifiable. But it is likely, even if the supposition of the memory box were true, that the mind can play tricks with those traces of the past, or that under the influence of a powerful drug Dick's sense of the distinctions between actuality, memory, and hallucination could become blurred. Dick cannot bear to think that the powerful link he feels with Roger Kylmerth is anything less than the truth. He desperately wishes to believe that the medieval world he has reached is at least as real as his own mundane environment. He has fallen in love with Isolda, and even if she can never feel his presence, he needs to keep their trysts across time.

I strongly suspect that there was a highly personal dimension to Daphne's exploration of Dick's mental state. Her letters to her friend Oriel Malet in the years leading up to the writing of *The House on the Strand* in 1968 reveal her fear of losing her creative powers. After her husband died in 1965, the possible forfeit of Menabilly after a quarter of a century hung over her while Philip Rashleigh changed his mind about the renewal of her lease. Her correspondence hinted at a worrying loss of a different sort: she confessed herself unable to 'brew' a new novel. *Vanishing Cornwall*, published in 1967, had been a kind of stop-gap, enabling her to work with her son, a photographer, on an illustrated project that depended on research rather than inspiration. The move to Kilmarth had stirred something in her, releasing her inventiveness once more in the devising of *The House on the Strand*, but the novel showed her continuing anxieties about the world of the imagination. What controlled access to that other life? Could she be shut out again, this time irrevocably?

Daphne the writer has two alter egos in *The House on the Strand*. One is Magnus, the magician who prepares the potion to take his disciple and himself into another realm. Dick feels apprehensive about the nature of Magnus's powers, referring to his basement laboratory as Bluebeard's den and reliving childhood nightmares engendered long ago by an engraving entitled 'The Alchemist':

> *A figure, naked save for a loincloth, was crouching by a walled oven like the one here in the laundry, kindling a fire with bellows, and to his left stood a hooded monk and an abbot, carrying a cross ... There had been bottles, too ... and in the flask a minute lizard with a dragon's head.* (Ch. 2, p.23)

Alchemists searching for the secret of making gold enter into strange alliances in their fanatical quests. They have a certain resemblance to writers like Daphne, who are delvers into the dark side of the psyche and stir the bubbling cauldrons of fiction with little certainty as to what will emerge from their unholy concoctions.

I suggest, however, that we find an even more significant alter ego for Daphne in the book's protagonist, Dick Young. Her fascination with his inner time travel between the present and the past can be seen as expressing her own anxieties about the switch that writers have to make repeatedly, as a condition of their being able to work at all, between the everyday world and the land of the imagination. The desire, even the necessity, for immersion in a vividly imagined other place, separate from the household and society within which we supposedly conduct our lives, had always given Daphne her greatest conviction that life was worth living. When she was in the middle of 'brewing' a book, as her children have testified, she was occupying a different space from the family around her. In the days of writing *Rebecca*, back in the 1930s, she had dazzled the senior editor at Gollancz, Norman Collins, with her creative energy: 'I don't know another author,' he wrote, 'who imagines so hard all the time.' But thirty years on, Daphne was beginning to panic that her powers were drying up. Dick's desperation about returning to the realm of Isolda, despite his growing awareness of the dangers of moving between the two ages, seems to be a way of expressing the fears of the author herself. Daphne felt that she had her own trysts with her imagination to keep, and she was not sure that she could survive psychologically without them.

Having reached the end of Part 2 of this reader's guide, we find ourselves at a remarkably similar point to the end of Part 1. We are once again talking about the author's relationship to her art, prompted into that discussion by ideas that bubble up from the undercurrents of her fiction. Daphne's fascination with what it means to be a writer is, for me, an important and enduring subject of her work.

What exactly is this imagined space which novelists create for readers to enter? How does this risky act of imagining happen, or not happen, and which is more frightening – being enveloped in the thrilling realm of fiction, or being excluded? And what is it worth, this risky act of imagining? More or less than the practical business of living and forming human bonds? Novels give no answers to such complex questions, but they can strike sparks which will continue to smoulder in our thoughts.

PART 3

THREE TALES OF TERROR

Introduction

If you've read this far but still cling to an idea of Daphne du Maurier as a romantic writer – don't look now! Daphne admitted to having macabre tastes, and gave them free rein in her short fiction. She writes about people who have selfish desires, psychic powers, hidden secrets or psychopathic obsessions. But she also deals in the unprepossessing behaviour of everyman and everywoman (everyman especially), and the disappointments and deceptions of daily lives.

A late story called 'No Motive', modelled on a traditional Agatha Christie country house murder mystery, begins with the butler's discovery that Lady Farren has shot herself in the gun room. The private detective hired to determine the motive for this shocking and inexplicable suicide follows the clues back to Lady Farren's childhood, exposing a chain of ordinary people covering up ordinary weaknesses, the stuff of minor crime and local scandal. 'It was always the way,' he observes. 'Temptation came to a man or woman, and they succumbed to it.'

In the weird tale of 'The Blue Lenses', temporary damage to the optic nerves after a major eye operation gives a woman insight as well as sight; the patient appears to be endowed with extraordinary vision, enabling her to see everyone around her as they really are. Each person she encounters, as in a kind of morality play, has the head of the creature that best fits their nature. Ominously, the nurse booked to attend her at home is a poisonous snake, and her own husband has the bloody beak of a vulture. We never know whether these insights are true or the result of the patient's paranoia – trapped as we are, du Maurier style, in one person's head – but such a bleak view of people's capacity for cruelty and betrayal darkens page after page of Daphne's short fiction.

Writing stories was the way Daphne learned her craft as a young author, and a large hardcover notebook she filled in her late teens, which is part of the fascinating collection held in the University of Exeter's archives, graphically demonstrates how hard she worked. The first pages in this notebook, dated May 1923 – the month that Daphne turned 16 – are written in ink, in a rather childish hand; the rest, dated three years later – the year that the du Mauriers found their Cornish house in Fowey, and Daphne found a new world for her imagination to range in – are consistently drafted in pencil, a habit which she followed for the rest of her career. Her method was to produce a single page of notes for each story, before writing it out in full at a later date. Her approach was professional and self-critical, and she was prepared to abandon mid-way a piece that was going wrong. Underneath one unfinished story entitled 'South Kensington', describing an upper-class wife at a dinner party, she has written 'Boring'; her first attempt at 'Top of a Bus', about the courtship of a servant who has lost her job, is condemned with the words: 'No, I don't think it would be good to write it like this, [it's] too easy and like a story in a cheap mag.' 'Top of a Bus' went better the second time, and she managed to finish this version.

Daphne set herself imaginative challenges to explore the mindset of people of vastly different ages and social backgrounds: a prostitute, a mentally disabled village girl, a snobbish vicar whose cold advice brings about a pregnant woman's suicide, a child terrified by the dark, an old man dependent on his daughters, a Breton grandmother who overhears her son wishing her dead. She is especially fascinated by the unspoken tensions in marriages, the repressed lives of suburban couples, and the inadequacies of men – marital cheats, child murderers, or merely losers. Four pages of notes bear the blunt heading, 'The Story of a Weak Man'. For a protected young writer from a privileged class background, her creative ambition is striking; and so is the depth of her teenage disillusion.

Daphne continued to experiment with the genre of the short story throughout her writing career, returning to the same themes with different treatments. Some fifty of her tales, many of them long enough to be classified as novellas, went into print. In the following pages we will look more closely at two stories from her fertile post-war period, 'The Birds' and 'Monte Verità', and at 'Don't Look Now', a compelling story written twenty years later, which was turned into a powerful film.

WARNING!

Read the stories and make your notes before looking ahead!

The Birds and **Monte Verità**
in *The Apple Tree* (1952)
or in *The Birds and Other Stories*
republished by Virago (2004)

Don't Look Now
in *Not After Midnight* (1971)
or in *Don't Look Now*
Penguin (1973 & 2006)

1 *The Birds*

On December the third the wind changed overnight and it was winter.

'The Birds' is a chilling tale, deriving much of its force from the simplicity of its telling. Many of du Maurier's stories depend on clever science fiction devices or dramatic Gothic effects, but here, from the spare elegance of its bleak opening lines, the mode is one of terse realism. The only unusual premise that the reader has to accept is that 'Something has happened to the birds.'

Daphne presents her main character in a single economical sentence:

Nat Hocken, because of a war-time disability, had a pension and did not work full-time at the farm.

Nat's war-time service and agricultural background, conveyed in those few introductory words, prepare us for his determined and practical response to the avian invasion, as the birds, from the largest gulls and gannets to the smallest larks and domestic wrens, embark on hostilities against the human population. While the farming way of life that provides the story's backdrop is traditional, this early reference to the recent war makes clear that the story is firmly set in a contemporary Britain of council housing and post-war recovery. The Second World War also creates a ready-made sense of communities under threat as the country faces a dire new crisis. When the birds start attacking, Nat thinks of the terrible raids on Plymouth, and turns his cottage kitchen into an air-raid shelter, where he and his wife tune in to wireless broadcasts from the BBC in London. But the birds are harder than German bombers to keep at bay, and the government and the armed forces seem to be powerless against this unexpected enemy. When the wireless falls silent, the killer birds are presumed to have invaded the national broadcasting centre with the ghastly consequences we have seen at the neighbouring farm. Meanwhile Nat stalwartly tries to keep his family safe in their old cottage, which has become a bunker against the pitiless forces ranged outside. Every stark detail brings home the few choices left to the isolated family as food and fuel start to run out and the wireless batteries fade. An oversight that lets the fire die away almost allows the birds to get down the kitchen chimney, and the doors and windows are being besieged as Nat reaches for his last cigarette.

By locating his version of 'The Birds' in California, Hitchcock lost much of the story's original impact, which drew on Daphne's reimagining of Cornish coastal farmland around Menabilly. It was while walking on Gribben Head that she had watched the gulls circling after a farmer's plough and conceived the idea of the murderous birds. She fully understood how farmers' livelihoods depended on uncontrollable weather and seasonal cycles, and having experienced a quarter of a century so close to the sea, she held no illusions about the devastating power of the elements or the relentless forces of the natural world. In 'The Birds' she writes with a sure touch about the significance of the change from 'the storm and bluster of a sou'westerly gale, bringing the rain,' to an unusually icy east wind, 'cold and dry' (p.3), which strips the trees 'like a razor' (p.7). Her plot makes play with tidal rhythms, as the gulls' instinctive withdrawal at the turning of the tide provides brief respites for Nat to make his careful preparations against the birds' renewed assault.

Daphne's post-war readers, with memories of recent hardships fresh in their minds, would have had no difficulty in empathising with the plight of Nat and his family under bombardment. But today's readers might interpret the story differently. 'The Birds' blames the southward shift of a cold Arctic air-stream for the birds' aggression; nature reacts with Darwinian adaptability, re-programming their behaviour, so that the creatures act with a new combined purpose and turn on humanity. In these days of uncontrollable climate change and the threat of a global pandemic caused by avian disease, the frightening hypothesis that a meteorological or epidemiological quirk might have unforeseen and devastating consequences is only too easy to believe. If horror in literature and film is about representing the nightmares of the age that society is refusing to contemplate, Daphne du Maurier's fifty-year-old scenario might be read as the ultimate horror story for the twenty-first century.

2 Monte Verità

'I love you, and have always loved you. Isn't that enough?' I asked.
'No,' she said, 'not on Monte Verità.'
And she threw back her cowl and I saw her face.
I gazed at her in horror . . . I could not move, I could not speak. It was as though all feeling had been frozen. My heart was cold . . . One side of her face was eaten quite away, ravaged, terrible. The disease had come upon her brow, her cheek, her throat, blotching, searing the skin. The eyes that I had loved were blackened, sunk deep into the sockets.
'You see,' she said, 'it isn't Paradise.' (p.110; author's punctuation)

In this self-consciously Gothic scene, the priestess, Anna, stands in a long tradition of mysteriously draped figures in monastic settings who throw back their cloaks to reveal some ghastly transfiguration. The grandfather of all Gothic novelists, Horace Walpole, described the ur-scene of hooded horror in *The Castle of Otranto* (1765). Frederic, suitor of the lovely Matilda, enters an oratory to seek the assistance of a woman he believes to be at prayer:

> *Pushing open the door gently, he saw a person kneeling before the altar ... [The] figure, turning slowly round, discovered to Frederic the fleshless jaws and empty sockets of a skeleton, wrapped in a hermit's cowl ...*

Frederic appeals to the spectre: *'But say, blest spirit, what is thy errand to me? what remains to be done?'*, only to receive a distressing reply:

> *'To forget Matilda!' said the apparition – and vanished.*

Such heart-stopping moments are the stuff of nightmare, and translate wonderfully onto the screen, with the shocked viewer standing in the place of the mesmerised victim. But the significance of these revelatory scenes is specific to each instance. When Anna appears in her sacred robes on Monte Verità before the man who has always loved her, after decades of separation, he has to learn a lesson as chilling as Frederic's: that he must forget Anna and his unreachable dream. But if we want to say any more about the meaning of Anna's disfigurement, we have to look closely at the precise web of possibilities that Daphne has woven around her.

We reach this climactic passage as the tale nears its end. Anna has become a high priestess of a strange sect, which carries out its rituals in a remote fortress on the Mountain of Truth. Many years earlier, a beautiful young woman, she disappeared from her husband's side on a walking holiday, only to be discovered at the monastery. She was radiantly happy with her new life but strikingly changed in appearance, dressed in the plain tunic of the cult with her natural abundance of golden hair cut short like a boy's. Now half a lifetime has passed, and the narrator (another of Daphne's fastidious bachelors) has climbed the peak to deliver a letter from her dying husband. The narrator had fallen in love with Anna at their first meeting, when they found that they shared a mutually understood need to search for spiritual truth, but had never declared his feelings. On this visit he is snatched into the fortress, where he sees Anna in her robes performing an initiation ceremony by cutting the hair of a neophyte, a village girl whose disappearance will prompt an assault on the monastery by the peasants. Then, as he appeals to her to let him help the community escape and spend her life with him, she turns ... and his dream is lost for ever.

Unlike other Gothic writers, who are inclined to use religious paraphernalia merely to create a vaguely supernatural aura, Daphne was intrigued by religious retreats and the promise of a spiritual life – indeed, one observant friend (Noël Welch, writing in the *Cornish Review*) saw 'something of the recluse in her, something of the monk.' *The Scapegoat*, written only a few years later, polarises an austere scholarly existence against a more selfish and sensual life, beginning and ending with the protagonist's plans for a sojourn in a Cistercian monastery, which may help him to understand what is worth living for. In 'Monte Verità' the narrator feels that his years of worldly success have missed the real point of life, which might have been the culmination of a quest that led him as a young man to seek the silent beauty of the mountains. But as he tells his story, he remains agnostic on whether the claims of the religion embraced by Anna are true. When the angry villagers destroy the monastery and find it deserted, have the inhabitants thrown themselves down

Alfred Hitchcock's THE BIRDS *(1963)*

Starring Tippi Hedren and Rod Taylor

Filmed in the open spaces of Bodega Bay on the California coast, Hitchcock's colour film has a very different feel to du Maurier's claustrophobic tale. Inevitably, this Hollywood movie is turned into a love story, with Hedren as a blonde socialite having to contend with two femme fatales in the form of Mitch's beautiful mother and brunette ex-mistress before she can stand by her man.

There are some moments of terror comparable to the original narrative – Hedren is trapped by gulls in a telephone box, black crows mass outside the local school, and the family is besieged in their lakeside house. The film also keeps du Maurier's war-time parallels: an aerial bird's-eye view of a garage forecourt going up in flames suggests a bomber pilot's perspective on a raid. There are dire predictions of the end of the world, though the audience is more likely to have the cold war and global nuclear destruction in mind than the Second World War. But despite the more graphic scenes of violence, the film is finally less bleak than Daphne du Maurier's tense story.

Nicholas Roeg's DON'T LOOK NOW *(1973)*

starring Donald Sutherland and Julie Christie

In Roeg's visually stunning film, the Baxters' little daughter drowns in a pond at her home, allowing the director to stir memories of her death with watery reflections in Venetian canals. The bright orange-red of the mac she is wearing when she dies recurs in splashes of the same lurid colour in scene after scene, finally becoming the colour of the dwarf's hooded coat, John's blood and the flowers on his funeral cortège.

The audience gets a very different insight into the Baxters' marriage through a tender and (for the time) explicit scene of love-making, bridging the emotional distance between the couple. But John deteriorates psychologically after Laura's departure. Venice grows sinister, foretelling the violence of the impending murder and the emptiness of death. In a dramatic sequence, John is drawn deeper into the labyrinth of Venice's dark, misty alleys in desperate pursuit of the wearer of the scarlet coat.

the chasm in a mass suicide pact, as seems only too likely, or fled from the mountain to hide themselves in civilian life? Or is there a further possibility open, that they have been transported straight to heaven?

Outside the sect, it was thought that devotees would never lose their youth or beauty, and Anna herself seems to have expected to find her paradise on the Mountain of Truth. Her leprous face undermines that tenet. And yet the monks of the spiritual citadel are full of joy, and Anna herself, despite the mortification of her flesh, appears to believe with as much conviction as before in a new truth without illusions. In other words, in the matter of faith, the story is not prepared to draw rational conclusions.

In its personal dimension, the plot has built up to the terrible moment of revelation with the narrator's growing sense that his inchoate desires will be at last focused and fulfilled. He feels, ecstatically, that his life will be utterly transformed by taking Anna as his lover and soul mate, and sharing the same spiritual path, and he chooses not to hear the lesson that Anna tries to teach him through her homely parable, as a way of preparing him for the changes in herself:

> *'There was once a man,' she said, 'who went to the booking office at Waterloo and said to the clerk eagerly, hopefully, "I want a ticket to Paradise. A single ticket. No return." And when the clerk told him there was no such place the man picked up the ink-well and threw it in the clerk's face.'* (p.109)

His romantic dreams are shattered by her diseased body – and so another of Daphne's yearning suitors is cruelly denied his happy-ever-after. But maybe the idea of some ineffable Truth, beyond any paradise on earth, survives undefaced.

If the secret exists, it is the woman, not the man, who holds it. Anna, with her cropped boyish hair, has embraced celibacy on entering the monastery, but instead of experiencing her renunciation as a bitter wrench, she has somehow been empowered in her quest for enlightenment. This androgynous figure in her sacred robes may, after all, have found the key to an elusive truth on which the narrator, still wishing for rapture on earth, can only speculate.

3 Don't Look Now

'Don't look now,' John said to his wife, 'but there are a couple of old girls two tables away who are trying to hypnotise me.'

This disturbing story about a married couple on holiday in Venice, trying to get back to some normality after their small daughter's death, is dominated from the opening lines by the controlling voice of the husband. His wife, Laura, obediently responds, 'quick on cue', entering into his banter and sneaking a surreptitious glance at the strange, grey-haired twins. But the reader does not become privy to her inner feelings except when she expresses them aloud; meanwhile, subjected to John's prejudiced viewpoint, we quickly becomes critical of his glib and somewhat misogynistic sense of superiority. When he thinks that one of the women is looking straight at him, not realising that she is blind, he immaturely attempts to out-stare her 'oddly penetrating' gaze: 'He blew a cloud of cigarette smoke into the air and smiled at her, he hoped offensively.' However, his impudent hostility begins to look faintly ridiculous: 'She did not register. The blue eyes continued to hold his, so that he was obliged to look away himself, extinguish his cigarette' (p.10). Though he never succeeds in imposing his opinions on his wife, or the elderly twins, John persists through the unsettling hours that follow in keeping to the high ground of rationality. He continues to resist the blind seer's premonitions, and his wife's emotional responsiveness (incidentally helping to undermine the scepticism of the reader by providing a sardonic filter for the emerging psychic theme). It is his voice that we hear to the very last words of the story, and only then, too late, does he realise that his own deafness and blindness have cost him his life.

'Don't Look Now' moves ahead at a terrific pace. Glancing through its pages and comparing it with the layout of 'The Birds', you can see that one explanation for its speed is the proportion of the story that consists of speech. The predominance of dialogue is already shifting the narrative in the direction of a film script, suggesting how readily it could be adapted to the screen. Daphne's visual moments also ask to be captured on camera – John's mood on his wife's hurried departure, for example, is caught with a few skilful close-up shots of the hotel room:

> *Laura's suitcases on the bed, a second coat she had left behind. Traces of powder on the dressing-table. A tissue, with a lipstick smear, thrown in the waste-paper basket.* (p.32)

The detail of the 'second coat' is both intimate in itself, and significant in the tapestry of the story. Laura is wearing her other coat, the scarlet one, when she says her last goodbye to John, and it is the eye-catching colour that focuses his attention in the clear premonitory vision he has of his wife passing him on a ferry boat with the two weird sisters.

The decaying canals and backstreets of Venice are a gift to writers and movie makers, and it takes a mere glimpse of its waterfront for Daphne to set up a Jekyll-and-Hyde contrast of day and night which raises the hairs on the back of the reader's neck:

> *The canal was narrow, the houses on either side seemed to close in upon it, and in the daytime ... there had been an impression of warmth, of secluded shelter. Now, ill-lit, almost in darkness, the windows of the houses shuttered, the water dank, the scene appeared altogether different, neglected, poor, and the long narrow boats moored to the slippery steps of cellar entrances looked like coffins.* (p.21)

The description prepares us for our first intimation of the bloodcurdling murders on which the plot's outcome depends, as the couple hear a terrible choking cry.

Visconti's film of Thomas Mann's *Death in Venice*, released in the same year as the publication of 'Don't Look Now' (1971), plays on the city's associations with homosexuality, and Daphne was only too willing to do the same. Within the du Maurier family circle, Venetian was the code word for lesbian. ('I only hope I haven't got Venetian tendencies', she wrote in her teens, about an infatuation with a French teacher.) She was equally sensitive to Venice's link with male homosexuality, and in a story entitled 'Ganymede'

(1959) she ironically used two locations, the Italian tourist city and the seedy district near London's Paddington Station known as 'Little Venice'.

When the married couple in 'Don't Look Now' amuse themselves with private quips about the sexual orientation of the two women at the next table, lesbianism is the most obvious target. Since it was an innuendo that tended to shadow any spinsters living together in the mid-twentieth century, the idea might already have occurred to contemporary readers. John and Laura's more fantastic speculations about the women being 'male twins in drag,' or 'criminals, doing the sights of Europe, changing sex at each stop' (p.9), are meant as crude jokes, but their words somehow accrue a more sinister patina from the story's Venetian setting. A sense of repulsion at the idea of physically unattractive older women having sex at all is surely one of the sources of such humour, which resurfaces in a vengeful manner at the dénouement of the narrative. The spine-chilling transformation of a fresh young girl into a deformed old dwarf in the final scene is a way of reconfiguring that disgust in a more perverted shape.

For, as the taut plot reaches its climax, the child John thinks he has been following for her protection is revealed to be a murderous dwarf. He has imagined the figure in the pixie-hood to be five or six, the same age as his lost daughter. The connection between the two figures is even clearer in the imagery of Nicolas Roeg's film, where the elusive child wears an orange-red coat – a splash of vivid youth, and of blood. Throughout the story, John has been the one superficially in control of his emotions, trying to distract Laura from her excessive mourning for their daughter. But the couple's suppressed grief has remained the powerful force which underlies the narrative. The way in which this child-like figure catches John's imagination and draws out his protectiveness, shows that deep down he has held on to his little girl.

John has been fatally mistaken in denying the insights of the blind old girl he belittled, whereas Laura felt their truth. The weird sister was right to predict that tragedy would strike in Venice, and right to detect John's latent psychic powers, which enable him to see his wife on the water with the two women after his own death. The tables have been turned on John in the cruellest fashion, and Laura, whose instincts have proved stronger than his determined rationality, will outlive him. He sees before him in his last moments the futility of his own end – 'a bloody silly way to die' – but there is something almost tragic about his inevitable fate, brought about through his own 'blind' arrogance. As the child he has loved is transformed into a hateful old woman, his repressed feelings conjure up a terrible nemesis in mythical shape. The moment of the 'pixie-hood falling from her head on to the floor' is a modern reworking of that old Gothic scene that reveals what the cowl has concealed. An old woman, a female dwarf with grey shoulder-length hair, the most horrible embodiment of death that John could envisage, is grinning at him, and pulling out her knife …

In our discussion of these three famous du Maurier stories, we have found ourselves in places that we recognise. The Cornish coastal setting of 'The Birds', the monastic retreat of 'Monte Verità', the tourist restaurants of 'Don't Look Now' and Venice's menacing back alleys, are familiar territory to readers of Daphne's fiction. In previous books, we have encountered similar men to the narrator of 'Monte Verità', longing for an unattainable woman, and witnessed cases of family trauma as anguishing as John and Laura's bereavement. But the intensified form of the short story seems to have licensed Daphne to explore the very darkest nooks of the psyche. The unsettling vision of human nature that pervades all her collections means that you are more likely to find paranoia or perversion than humour or happiness. But if you dare to read on, you will also encounter some of her most brilliant writing.

PART 4

IT'S ONLY THE SISTER

Angela du Maurier

We know many of the du Mauriers from the colourful portraits in Daphne's own writing, from her *Punch* grandfather and her actor father, to her French ancestors and her Peter Pan cousins. But there are two members of her immediate family who have been in danger of dropping from sight – her talented sisters. Daphne's elder sibling, Angela, was a writer, who came down to live in Cornwall with her mother and stayed on, with her beloved Pekinese dogs, in an increasingly decrepit and creeper-covered Ferryside, until she moved into a nursing home at the age of 91. Her younger sister, Jeanne, was a painter, who once had her own studio in St Ives where she became a lifelong friend of the artist Dod Procter. Jeanne's paintings can be found in several galleries and private collections, but her greatest legacy is her lovely Devon longhouse with its gardens merging into Dartmoor. Half Moon evolved over forty years, the shared creation of Jeanne and the poet Noël Welch.

'Sisters?' wrote Noël boldly in the vibrant 'little magazine', the *Cornish Review*. 'They should have been brothers. They would have made splendid boys.' But here the resemblance between the three women seems to end, and Noel's account of Angela's cheerful socialising, efficiently organised travelling, political campaigning and insistence on her rights as eldest sibling ('Esauing', Daphne called it) throw into relief Jeanne's retreat to Dartmoor and Daphne's to Cornwall. If Angela was the active sister, Daphne was the contemplative one:

> *[Angela] is an excellent speaker and always ready to open fêtes – one could get Daphne to the stake more easily than to the opening of a fête.*

Angela became ensconced in Fowey, high Tory, high Anglican, and respected godmother to several children, though her later reputation for probity was belied by her continuing appetite for scandal and her enduring sense of fun.

Writing when Angela was in her sixties, Noël hinted slyly:

Angela is the most conventional [of the three sisters] now but I have seen photographs, curled at the edges, blurred and hastily snatched away, showing a wilder Angela than the one I know [–] though sometimes in a sudden flash of humour, a ribald remark, one gets glimpses of a Bohemian past.

Her delightful memoir, self-mockingly entitled *It's Only the Sister*, is a fresh first-hand account of the du Maurier girls' busy social life in the twenties – the 1920s, that is, and also the early twenties of Angela and Daphne. Keeping up with Angela in top gear leaves you breathless – she was a fast driver and formidable traveller – as she whisks the reader from skating parties in Geneva to artists' studios on the Left Bank, from the opera house at Covent Garden to centre court at Wimbledon. She even made occasional minor stage appearances, notably in the role of Wendy in that hallmark du Maurier production, *Peter Pan*. Angela's friends were many and varied, including of course ramifications of the family's theatrical circle. As a young woman, Daphne had access to the same milieu – in the winter of 1929, for example, while partying nightly at the Swiss ski resort of Caux, she met Carol Reed, with whom she shortly began an affair. Yet most of the time it is hard to believe that the sisters were living the same life, as Daphne's need for solitude, and her more cynical attitude towards the society she moved in, drew her to the edges of the crowd that made her elder sister happy.

Angela loved Fowey and lived in Ferryside until her extreme old age, but her recollections of Cornwall are bathed in a different imaginative light to Daphne's. Comparing the treatment of their first sight of the River Fowey, in their respective memoirs, we find that Daphne's immediate desire was to escape her family in order to enjoy this peaceful place alone, whereas Angela's account taken from her diary at the time, is enthusiastically noisy and companionable:

Motored to Fowey which we fell in love with directly. To Bodinnick first, ***adorable****. Unfortunately could not get into the Inn there. Saw over perfect little place to be sold ... Motor-boated to Polperro for tea, very nearly sick.* ***Quite*** *heaven on earth, no words to describe it. Motored back, perfect scenery.*

(Quoted in *It's Only The Sister*, p.121)

At Ferryside Daphne daydreamed about the river's past, as she wrote *The Loving Spirit*. Angela's Ferryside is very much in the present, the location of marvellous anecdotes, like the time when the actress Viola Tree (Carol Reed's half-sister) took an unplanned swim:

> *I always think the funniest occasion in my memories of Viola was the time she paid her first real visit to us, at Fowey, arriving one morning by motor-boat, and falling straight into the harbour, fully clothed and with a rather smart hat on her head. Utterly undaunted, and in full view of a number of people, including – naturally – Daddy, Viola turned tail and went for a swim, her smart hat becoming more and more rakish as the waves rippled it. That swim nearly cost her her life, for she caught a severe chill and within a week was desperately ill with acute peritonitis.* (p.47)

When Angela writes vividly on wartime Fowey in the 'forties, it's all about market gardening and the American marines, while in the same years Daphne is caught up with the personal demands of her growing family, her move to Menabilly, and the writing of *The King's General.*

For all three sisters, however, the inner life of the imagination and the spirit was as important, in the end, as the outer life. While Daphne seems to have remained agnostic – though always fascinated by spirituality – religion of a highly organised and orthodox kind was central to the lives of both her sisters. As Noël Welch explained, religion was important to Angela and Jeanne, whereas Daphne was a 'pagan'. According to *It's Only the Sister*, their father's family was 'allergic to church', while their mother's family was distinctly 'churchy', introducing young Angela to the emotional and theatrical experience of High Mass. The result was that Daphne followed more in the path of the unbelieving du Mauriers, but Jeanne became a Catholic, devoting one room of her Dartmoor home to a chapel and laying out the land behind the house as a Marian garden in honour of the Virgin. Angela became High Church, worshipping latterly not at her nearest parish church at Lanteglos, but at St Winnow, the beautiful creekside church that held more satisfyingly ritualistic services.

Several of Angela's books involve personal spiritual quests, featuring clergymen as leading characters in the vein of Victorian battle-of-belief novels. When they were first published, they were already behind the time in which they were written, and most of her fiction has subsequently dated in a way that does not apply to Daphne's work. But one particularly bold and vivid religious tale stands out, *The Road to Leenane*, which was inspired by Angela's intense spiritual experience of Ireland.

DAPHNE'S SISTERS

Angela du Maurier, Writer 1904–2001

Though Angela would not have described herself as a writer, she published thirteen books. Most of them are hard to obtain today, and The Little Less, *known as her 'lesbian novel', which describes in rather decorous terms the young heroine's attraction to 'menaces' of both sexes, can be priced around £100 on the second hand market. She also wrote two volumes of autobiography, a travel book, several religious novels and a collection of short stories.*

Truran Books has republished three of her best works: her Irish novel The Road to Leenane, *her tautly plotted Cornish romance* Treveryan, *written during the war in an intense creative break of two months on the island of Mull, and her sparkling memoir,* It's Only the Sister.

Jeanne du Maurier, Artist 1911–1997

(by Alison Oldham)

Jeanne would have described herself as a painter first and foremost. She was an oil painter influenced by the Impressionists, an intimiste who found many subjects in her home. One speciality was flower painting, another was still-life compositions with a musical motif: stringed instruments, scores and stands. Though she painted scenes outdoors on her own land and when travelling abroad, these pictures rarely include people even in townscapes.

The Royal West of England Academy, with whom Jeanne exhibited from the '50s onwards, has the largest public holding, including the fine 'Mimosa', with its orange and silver du Maurier cigarette box, and the almost abstract 'Bird Cage'. The best private collection is at Half Moon, the 12th-century longhouse where Jeanne lived with the poet Noël Welch from 1953. In the Cornish Review *in 1973, Noël wrote of Jeanne's painting: 'Her palette is high-keyed, her colour singing. She cares more for colour than form and is always fascinated by the reflection of her subject in the looking glass so often placed beside or behind the original.'*

To date, the most comprehensive record of Jeanne's career is in Creating a Splash, *David Tovey's history of the St Ives Society of Artists to which Jeanne belonged from 1945 to 1949. The entry includes a photograph of her, palette in hand, with her great friend, the Newlyn painter Dod Procter. Jeanne exhibited widely and many paintings are dispersed in private collections.*

The Road to Leenane

Set among the stunning scenery of Connemara, *The Road to Leenane* (1963) is plotted simply around five key characters. A young village girl, Paddy O'Malley, marries her childhood sweetheart, the painter and writer Micky Renvyle. They name their only daughter Killary, after Killary Harbour near Leenane where they spent their honeymoon. Paddy is talent-spotted by filmmakers on location and leaves Ireland for a successful career as an actress for stage and film, but since the couple are Catholics there is no prospect of divorce in the sight of the church. Micky is wedded to his Irish home, which is also the inspiration of his writing and artwork, and cannot face joining his wife permanently in London. As a good Catholic, he disapproves of contraception, and falls out of love with Paddy, who has been tempted away from her traditional Irish roots, when she confesses to an abortion. Angela's own passion for the stage did not prevent her from stereotyping the theatrical world as wicked for fictional purposes, giving the novel a resolutely old-fashioned air.

In Paddy's absence, Micky is involved with two women: Lady Constance, his larger-than-life Anglo-Irish benefactress, six feet tall, flamboyant and overbearing, and plain Joan, a bespectacled librarian, who wins the hearts of Micky and his daughter. Joan's unwavering Catholic faith keeps her physically apart from Micky, even when he obtains a legal divorce from his estranged wife, since in Joan's eyes only Paddy's death would enable him to re-marry. As Micky is drawn into cosmopolitan art circles and spends less time in his Irish home, Joan goes on retreat to the Convent of Mercy, on the road that leads from Killary Harbour up the valley to Leenane, and is slowly drawn towards the peace it affords.

The novel's unwavering sympathy with Catholicism does not seem to have represented Angela's personal opinion. She had been hostile to Jeanne's conversion, remaining firmly on the Anglican side of that passionately disputed line between the High Church and the Roman Church. But, though some individual characters argue for a bending of the rules, *The Road to Leenane* offers little serious criticism of the strictest Catholic position – rather the opposite, praising the inner peace bestowed by religious certainty. The logic of the plot, which holds its secrets until the final pages, relies on the immutable rules of the Catholic faith: no divorce, no abortion, no contraception, no living in sin. Though this may seem an outdated theme to most readers in Britain, and in today's Catholic Ireland, our reading context may be changing with the growth of faith communities in the west. Now that the debate about religious identity has been re-invigorated, making plots centred on moral and spiritual choice freshly available to a new generation of British writers, *The Road to Leenane* could become unexpectedly relevant to the twenty-first century.

Angela's characters act with an innocence that would make them entirely unfit to inhabit any of Daphne's imaginative worlds. Their faith is untroubled by doubt, their understanding of right and wrong clearly lit, their desires bounded. The reader may find their transparency incredible – and the extreme naivety of Micky's little girl can be particularly irritating at times – but they engage our interest and concern. The position of women is questioned when Paddy, the rebellious wife, abandons her home for the stage, but Angela opts to endorse the idealised view of a woman's traditional lot. The most intriguing character is plain Joan, who introduces the fascinating theme of the role of single women as they face the prospect of becoming elderly spinsters. (Angela of course realised that she herself was placed in the same category, and gave her second memoir the tongue-in-cheek title, *Old Maids Remember*.) Since the central conflict of the novel takes place within Joan, torn between carnal and spiritual love, we might regret that so much of the novel is told in dialogue, drawing a discreet veil over her inner torment. Had Daphne told a similar story, the guilt, the desire and the agonising would absorb our attention, with mere dialogue masking rather than manifesting the stormy state of Joan's psyche. And Daphne would certainly have considered writing the story in the first person, allowing deeper immersion in the narrator's thoughts and feelings. But would she have taken the viewpoint of the ageing woman, like Honor Harris in *The King's General*, I wonder? I rather suspect that she would have decided to stand in the shoes of the weaker man, torn between three women and God.

It is in fact the very innocence of *The Road to Leenane* that makes it such a compelling read. It is also successful in underpinning the story with one symbolic place. Much-travelled Angela admitted to love affairs with many locations. 'To fall in love with a place,' she confessed, 'is as exciting as to fall in love with a human being. I have done both, and often' (*Old Maids Remember*, p.79). A remote house on the Island of Mull, described in *It's Only the Sister*, is perhaps her equivalent of Jeanne's Half Moon and Daphne's Menabilly, but it was an utterly unforeseen midlife experience of Connemara, she writes in *Old Maids Remember*, that struck the most thrilling chord:

> *above all and for ever the desolate road to Leenane and Killary Harbour … has for me something I have never met or known before. There was a peace about that road and the stark hills which guard it that I believe one might know at death; for me it was as if one suddenly came face to face with a vision of Himself and all He has to give … [My] road to Leenane … is prayer itself … akin to the bridegroom's feeling of wonder when his beloved lifts her veil and he knows at last the meaning of eternity.* (p.87)

In the novel, the road to Leenane comes to symbolise the two paths of life, to earthly or spiritual happiness. On the one hand, Killary is the emblem of romance and marriage, and the name given to a child; on the other, the way leading to the Convent of Mercy promises serenity to a bride of Christ. It is part of Angela's achievement that the modern reader finds it as hard as the heroine to decide which is the better path.

PART 5

EAST WIND

Introduction

One of the most atmospheric pieces in Daphne du Maurier's 1926 notebook, held by the University of Exeter, is 'East Wind', set on a remote island beyond the Scillies. Nearly fifty years later, writing in the *Cornish Review*, Noel Welch was to note Daphne's 'obsession with the sea and the tide', even claiming that: 'It is at high tide that her stories are always begun.' This gripping yarn shows how strongly, even as a teenager, she felt the compulsion of the sea.

The story was composed when Daphne was 19, and working hard at her chosen métier. Taking up thirty pages of her notebook, her pencil draft appears to have been written rapidly, with only light corrections. When she copied it out she noted in her diary:

> *Few people will read it or like it. There's no converstion at all, a few scattered sentences. I don't know if I've caught the atmosphere or not. It's sordid, perhaps, brutal, and essentially primative.*

This is apprentice work, melodramatic and prone to cliché, but the tale has a crude imaginative power that makes it an enthralling read. And for readers familiar with Daphne's published work, this roughly crafted piece gives a fascinating insight into the fiction to come.

Daphne already knew the maritime regions of Brittany and Cornwall, which feature elsewhere in her teenage writing. In 1926, she spent part of her summer in France, swimming on the coast of Brittany with her former French teacher, and the end of the season in Cornwall. But for 'East Wind' she imagined an even more isolated fishing community in the days before wireless communication, where the livelihood of the inhabitants is at the mercy of the waves.

The plot of 'East Wind' depends on a change in the weather. Once the slow opening paragraphs have established the community's monotonous way of life, a break in the villagers' routine is signalled by the impending easterly wind. The high pressure is set to bring days of unremittingly clear skies, which dry out the soil, and rough seas 'angrier than the devil', which keep the fishing boats on their moorings. The islanders wake one morning to find a foreign brig seeking shelter in their harbour, crewed by dark, slant-eyed sailors, who bring potent brandy for the men and coloured scarves for their wives. As the exotic visitors disrupt the customary life of the village with their liquor and womanising, the relentless wind is likened to 'a demon let loose upon the island' and a scorching 'breath from Hell.' The tension builds as the easterly whips the islanders into an anarchic frenzy.

Sex, violence, and the sea – here we have the elements of du Maurier's distinctive adult work! And when the central female figure of the story, Guthrie's wife Jane, kneels by her bedroom window, longing *to creep from the cottage and run onto the cliffs, where she would feel the true force of the wind,* we recognise a prototype of all those characters, as yet unwritten, whose unfulfilled desires threaten to destroy the contentment of their mundane existence.

Three years after writing 'East Wind', on 3rd October 1929, the young author sat down at her desk in Ferryside to commit the heroine of her first novel to paper. Janet Coombe, a lover of the cliffs and the wild seas, is a recognisable successor to Guthrie's wife in 'East Wind'. But Daphne was embarking on a far more ambitious project, and ready to create a complex character who could develop over many chapters. As she fully recognised, at that moment there was a lot at stake. Her apprenticeship was over and her professional career was about to begin.

East Wind

Nearly a hundred miles west of the Scillies, and far from the main track of ships, lies the small rocky island of St. Hilda's.

Only a few miles square, it is a barren rugged sort of a place, with great jagged cliffs that run steep into deep water.

The harbour is hardly more than a creek, and the entrance is like a black hole cut out of the rock. The island rises out of the sea, a queer mis-shapen crag, splendid in its desolation, with a grey face lifted to the four winds. It might have been thrown up from the depths of the Atlantic in a moment of great unrest, and set there, a small defiant piece of land to withstand forever the anger of the sea.

Over a century ago few knew of its existence, and the many sailors who saw its black outline on the horizon imagined it to be little more than a solitary rock, standing like a sentinel in mid ocean.

The population of St. Hilda's has never exceeded seventy, and the people are descendants of the original settlers from the Scillies and Western Ireland.

Their only means of livelihood used to be the catching of fish, and the cultivation of the soil. Today things are greatly changed, owing to the monthly call of a coastal steamer, and the installation of wireless.

In the middle half of the last century years would sometimes pass without communication from the mainland, and the people had degenerated into quiet listless folk, the inevitable result of inter-marriage. There were no books then, no papers, and even the small chapel that had been built by the original settlers had fallen into disuse.

Year in, year out, the life remained unchanged, with never a new face or a fresh thought to break the monotony of the days. Sometimes, on the horizon, the faint glimmer of a sail would be seen, and the people would gaze with wonder in their eyes; but slowly the sail would become a far-off distant speck, and the unknown ship pass into oblivion.

They were peaceable folk, those natives of St. Hilda's, born to a quiet untroubled existence, as monotonous as the waves that broke against their shores. They knew nothing of the world beyond the island, they saw no greater happenings than birth, and death, and the changes of the seasons. Their lives were untouched by great emotions, by great sorrows, their desires had never been lit but lay imprisoned within their souls. They lived blindly, happily like children, content to grope in the dark, and never to search for the something that lay beyond their darkness. Some inner sense warned them that in their ignorance dwelt security, a happiness that was never wild, never triumphant, but peaceful and silent. They walked with their eyes to the ground; they had become weary of looking upon a sea where no ship came, of lifting their faces to a sky that seldom changed.

Summer and winter passed, children grew into men, there was no more in life than these things. Far away lay the other lands dwelt in by strange people, where the life was said to be hard and men had to fight for their existence. Sometimes an islander would sail away, shaping his course for the mainland, and promising to return with news of the rest of the world. Perhaps he would be drowned, or picked up by some passing ship; no one could say for he never came back. No one who left the island returned. Even the few ships that so rarely visited St. Hilda's came once only, passing not again.

It was almost as if there was no such place, as if the island was a dream, a phantom creation of a sailor's brain, something rising out of the sea at midnight as a challenge to reality. Then vanishing in surf and mist to be forgotten, to be half-consciously remembered years later, flickering for a bewildered second in a dusty brain, as a dead thought. Yet to the people of St. Hilda's the island was reality, the ships that came and went were their phantoms.

There was only the island. Beyond it lay the ghostly, the

intangible; the truth was in the scarred rock, in the touch of the soil, in the sound of the waves breaking against the cliffs. This was the belief of the humble fisherfolk, and they cast their nets during the day, and gossiped over the harbour wall at evening with never a thought of the lands across the sea. At dawn the men set off to fish, and when their nets were filled they would return to the island, and climb the steep path that led to the fields, to work with stolid patience at the soil.

The group of cottages were clustered together at the water's edge, with seldom more than two rooms to contain an entire family. Here the women bent over their fires and cooked, and darned their men's clothes, toiling peacefully from dawn till dusk.

One cottage stood apart from the others, built high on the cliff and looking down upon the creek. Today only the site remains, and instead of a cottage stands the ugly wireless station, but sixty years ago this was the home of the chief fisherman of St. Hilda's. Here Guthrie dwelt with his wife Jane, living neither passionately nor supremely, but as children content in each other, unmindful of desire, ignorant of distress.

Guthrie stood on the cliffs at twilight, watching the sea. Below him in the harbour the fishing boats rocked, moored for the night. The men gossiped over the harbour wall, the sound of their voices rose to him, mingled with the thin cries of children. The little quay was slippery with spray, and blood, and the scales of dead fish. The smoke curled from the chimneys, a thin blue column, twisting and turning in the air. From the door of his cottage came Jane, her hands to her eyes, searching for him.

"Come away down!" she called. "The supper's been ready an hour since. Ye'll find 'un spoilt, as likely as not." He waved his arm and turned, pausing to glance at the horizon for the last time. The sky was speckled with white loose-flocked clouds, and the sea, changed from the oily smoothness of the day, was running past the harbour in a low swell. Already there was a wash upon the rocks, at the eastward entrance. A soft humming sound came to his ears, as the sea gathered in force, and a cool breeze played with his hair. He ran down the hill to the village, and cried to the fishermen who were standing by the wall. " 'Tis the East wind startin'", he told them, "can't ye see the sky like a fish's tail, and the big lumpin' sea awash on the rocks? Before midnight there'll be a gale to blow your heads off, and the sea angrier than the devil himself. Look to the boats." The harbour was sheltered from the wind, yet the vessels were moored securely fore and aft to prevent the possibility of their breaking adrift.

After he had seen that everything was safe for the night, Guthrie climbed the path to his cottage on the cliff. He ate his supper in silence. He felt restless and excited, the quiet atmosphere of the cottage seemed to oppress him. He tried to occupy himself in mending a hole in one of his nets, but he could not give his mind to the task. The net slipped from his hands, he turned his head and listened. It seemed as if a cry had risen out of the night. Yet there was nothing, only the low hum of the wind, and the sound of surf breaking upon the rocks. He sighed and gazed into the fire, oddly disturbed, his soul heavy within him.

In the bedroom with her head by the window, Jane knelt, listening to the sea. Her heart beat strangely, her hands trembled, she wanted to creep from the cottage and run onto the cliffs, where she would feel the true force of the wind. It would strike upon her breast, and sweep the hair from her face, she would hear the singing of it in her ears, she would smell the salt tang of the spray as it stung her lips and her eyes.

The longing came upon her to laugh with the wind, to cry with the sea, to open wide her arms and be possessed by something unknown. She hated the night which enveloped her like a dark cloak, which prevented her from straying far away on the lonely cliffs amongst the tall grass. She prayed for the day to dawn, not gently as was its custom, but fiercely, with the sun burning the fields, and the wind sweeping the white-edged seas, bringing destruction. She would stand and wait upon the shore, feeling the wet sand beneath her naked feet.

A footstep sounded outside the room, she turned with a little shiver from the window. It was Guthrie. He gazed at her solemnly, and bade her shut out the sound of the wind. They undressed quietly, and lay beside each other in the narrow bed without a word. He could feel the warmth of her body, but his heart was not with her. His thoughts left his form, imprisoned there at her side, and fled into the night. She felt him go, yet minded not. She put away his cold dumb hands from her, and gave herself to her own dreams, where he could have no entrance.

Thus they slept together in each other's arms, yet separately; like dead things in a grave, their souls long vanished and forgotten.

When they awoke the dawn had broken in the sky. The sun shone blindly from a blue heaven, searching the earth. Great seas, tipped with foam, crashed against the cliff, and swept the rocks outside the harbour. And all the while the East wind blew, tossing the grass, scattering the hot white sand, forcing its triumphant path through the white mist and the green waves, like a demon let loose upon the island.

Guthrie went to the window and looked out upon the day. A cry came from his lips – he ran from the cottage, unable to believe his eyes. Jane followed him. The folk in the other cottages had risen too, and stood staring at the harbour, their hands lifted in amazement, their excited voices filling the air with sound, yet fading away, indistinguishable, borne by the wind.

For there in the harbour, dwarfing the little fishing boats with her great spars, the sails stretched upon her yards to dry in the morning sun, lay a brig at anchor, rocking against wind and tide.

Guthrie stood on the quay amongst the crowd of fishermen. The whole of St. Hilda's was gathered there to welcome the strangers from the brig. Tall dark men they were, these sailors from beyond the sea, with narrow almond eyes, and white teeth that gleamed as they laughed.

They spoke in a different tongue. Guthrie and his fellows questioned them, while the women and children surrounded them with gaping mouths, gazing into their faces, feeling their clothes with timid wondering hands. "How did ye find the entrance to the harbour," cried Guthrie, "with the wind an' the sea in league together against ye? 'Tis the Devil himself that hath sent ye here maybe."

The sailors laughed, and shook their heads. They could not understand what he said.

Their eyes wandered beyond him and the fishermen to the women, they smiled and spoke amongst themselves, happy at their discovery.

All the while the sun beat down upon their heads, and the East wind blew, scorching the air like a breath from Hell.

No man went forth to fish that day. Great mountainous seas thundered past the harbour mouth, and the fishing boats remained at anchor, small and insignificant beside the strange brig.

Something of madness seemed to fall upon the people of St. Hilda's. Their nets lay neglected and unmended beside their cottage doors, the fields and flowers remained untended on the hills above the village. There was no interest in their lives but the sailors from the ship. They clambered upon the brig, leaving no part of her unvisited, they touched the strangers' clothes with excited inquisitive fingers. The sailors laughed at them, they hunted in the sea chests and presented the men with cigarettes, they found bright scarves and coloured handkerchiefs for the women.

Guthrie led them out upon the cliffs, swaggering a little like a young boy, a cigarette between his lips.

The fishermen threw wide their cottage doors, jealous of each other's hospitality, each one desirous to extend the greatest welcome. The sailors soon explored the island; they thought it a poor barren place, empty of interest. They descended to the shore and formed themselves in groups on the quayside, yawning, idle, hoping for a change of weather. The time hung heavily upon their hands.

Still the East wind blew, scattering the sand, turning the earth to dust. The sun blazed from a cloudless sky, the big seas swept around the shores, green, foam-flecked, twisting and turning like a live thing.

The sun set streaky and wind-swept, pointing orange fingers to the sky. The night came, warm and alive. They very air was restless. The sailors found the disused chapel at the end of the village, and encamped themselves there, fetching tobacco and brandy from the brig.

There seemed to be no order amongst them, they had no discipline, they obeyed no rules. Two men only remained on the brig to watch. The fisherfolk wondered not at their conduct, their presence on the island was too wonderful and rare a thing. Nothing counted but this. They joined the sailors in the chapel, they tasted brandy [for] the first time. The night rang with cries and song. The island was a new place now, broken of peace, swayed by suggestion and filled with strange desires. Guthrie stood amongst his companions, his cheeks flushed, his cold eyes bright and foolish. He held a glass in his hand, he swallowed the brandy with deep contented draughts. He laughed with the sailors, wildly, without reason, what did it matter if he could not understand their words? The lights swayed before his eyes, the ground sloped beneath his feet. It seemed to him as if he had never lived before. The wind could shout, and the sea thunder and roar, the world called to him now. Beyond the island lay the other lands, the homes of these sailors. Here he would find life, and beauty, and strange incredible adventures. No more would he cast his nets into the weary waters of St. Hilda's, no more would he bend his back, toiling at the useless soil. The songs of the sailors rang in his ears, the tobacco smoke blinded his eyes, the brandy seemed to mix with the blood in his veins.

The women danced with the sailors. Someone had found a concertina, and a fiddle with three strings. Crazy tunes broke into the air. The women had never danced before. They were whirled from their feet, their petticoats flying out behind them. The sailors laughed and sang, beating the measure with their feet upon the floor. The fishermen lolled stupidly against the walls, drunken, happy, careless of time. A sailor came across to Jane, and smiled, holding out his arms. She danced with him, flushed, excited, eager to please. Faster, faster went the music, and faster flew their feet around the room.

She felt his arm tighten round her waist, and was aware of the warmth of his body against hers. She could feel his breath upon her cheek. She raised her head and met his eyes. They looked into her, seeing her naked. He moistened his lips with his tongue. They smiled, reading each other's thoughts. An exquisite shudder, like the touch of a cool hand, ran through her. Her legs felt weak beneath her. She lowered her eyes, conscious of desire, and turned to see if Guthrie had noticed, guilty for the first time.

And the East wind blew against the church, shaking the roof, and the surf broke and thundered on the shore.

The next day dawned the same, hot and relentless.

The wind did not weaken in its power, nor the sea lessen in its fury. The brig still rolled at her moorings amongst the fishing boats. The fishermen leant with the sailors against the harbour wall, drinking and smoking, without thought, without energy, cursing the wind. The women idled at their cooking, neglected their mending. They stood at the doors of the cottages, a new scarf round their shoulders, a scarlet handkerchief upon their heads, impatient with the children, restless, waiting for a smile.

The day passed thus, and another night, and yet another day. The sun shone, the sea shuddered and crashed, the wind blew. No one left the harbour to fish, no one worked on the land. There seemed no shade on the island, the grass lay brown and withered, the leaves hung parched and despondent from the few trees. Night fell once more, and the wind had not ceased.

Guthrie sat in the cottage, his head between his hands, his brain empty. He felt ill and tired, like a very old man. Only one thing could prevent the sound of the wind from screaming in his ears, and the heat of the sun from scorching his eyes.

His lungs were dry, his throat ached. He staggered from the cottage, and went down the hill to the church, where the sailors and the fishermen lay in heaps on the floor, the brandy running from their mouths. He flung himself amongst them, and drank greedily, senselessly, giving himself to it, forgetting the wind and the sea.

Jane closed the cottage door behind her, and ran out onto the cliffs. The tall grass bathed her ankles, and the wind leapt through her hair. It sang in her ears, a triumphant call. The sea flung itself upon the rocks below, loose flecks of foam scattered up towards her. She knew that if she waited he would come to her from the chapel. All the day his eyes had followed her, as she walked amongst the sailors by the harbour wall. Nothing mattered but this. Guthrie was drunk, asleep, forgotten, but here on the cliffs the stars shone upon her, and the East wind blew.

A dark shadow appeared from behind a clump of trees. For one moment she was afraid, one moment only.

"Who are you?" she called, but her voice fled with the wind.

The sailor came towards her. He flung off her clothes with deft accustomed fingers; she put her hands before her eyes to hide her face. He laughed, and buried his lips in her hair.

She stood then with her arms outstretched, waiting, naked and unashamed, like a white phantom, broken and swept by the wind. Down in the chapel the men shouted and sang. They fought amongst themselves, mad with drink. One fisherman threw a knife and pinned his brother against the wall. He writhed like a serpent, screaming with pain.

Guthrie rose to his feet.

"Quiet, you dogs," he shouted. "Can you not drink in peace, and leave men to their dreams? Is it like this you wait for the wind to change?"

Jeers and laughter drowned his voice. A man pointed a trembling finger at him.

"Aye – talk of peace, Guthrie, you weak-limbed fool. With your wife even now shaming your bed with a stranger. We'll have new blood in the island, I reckon." A chorus of voices joined in, laughing, and pointing at him.

"Aye, Guthrie, look to your wife."

He leapt at them with a cry of rage, smashing their faces. But they were too many for him, they threw him from the chapel, flinging him onto the rough quay side. He lay stunned for a moment, then shook himself like a dog, and rose to his feet. So Jane was a wanton, Jane had deceived him. He remembered his wife's body, white and slim. A haze of madness came over him, mingled with hatred and desire. He stumbled through the darkness, up the hill, to the cottage.

There was no light in any of the windows, the rooms were empty.

"Jane," he called, "Jane, where be ye hidin' with your damned cur lover?" No one answered.

Sobbing with rage he tore an axe from the wall. A great clumsy tool, used for chopping firewood.

"Jane," he called once more, "come out, will ye?"

His voice was powerless against the wind that shook the walls of the cottage. He crouched by the door and waited, the axe in his hands. Hours passed, and he sat in a stupor, awaiting her return. Before dawn she came, pale and trembling, like a lost thing. He heard her footfall on the path, a twig snapped under her. She crept into the cottage and saw him there, swaying upon his feet, the axe uplifted.

"Guthrie," she screamed, "Guthrie, let me alone, let me alone."

She spread out her hands in supplication, but he pushed them aside, and brought the axe down upon her head, crumpling her, smashing her skull. She fell to the ground, twisted, unrecognizable, ghastly.

He leant over her, peering at her body, breathing heavily. The blood ran before his eyes. He sat down by her side, his senses swimming, his mind vacant. He fell into a drunken sleep, his head pillowed on her breast.

When he awoke, sober, himself again, he found her dead body at his feet. He gazed at it in horror, not understanding. The axe lay upon the floor. He sat stunned, sick and frightened, unable to move. Then he listened, as if for an accustomed sound. All was silent. Something had changed, something had departed. The wind. He could no longer hear the wind.

He staggered to his feet, and looked out upon the island. The air was cool. Rain had fallen while he had slept. From the south-west blew a cool steady breeze. The sea was grey and calm. Far on the horizon lay a black dot, her white sails outlined against the sky.

The brig had gone with the morning tide.

This story – previously unpublished in the UK – is taken from a hardcover notebook (dated 1923 inside one cover, and 1926 inside the other) in the du Maurier archives held by Special Collections, Information Services, University of Exeter (EUL MS 144/1/1/1). The story consists of thirty sides of large handwriting, in pencil, at the 1926 end of the notebook. Spelling, punctuation and paragraphing have been corrected and standardised.

Places to go

Fowey is the centre of 'du Maurier country'. For up-to-date tourist information, and details of the Daphne du Maurier Festival of Arts and Literature, held every May see www.fowey.co.uk (tel. 01726 833616), and visit the dedicated Daphne du Maurier website at www.dumaurier.org.

The Daphne du Maurier Literary Centre in Fowey shows a video about Daphne in her Cornish context, and sells her books.

Ferryside is closed to the public, but the riverfront façade with the Jane Slade figurehead under an upper window can be seen as you cross from Fowey to Bodinnick on the car ferry.

Menabilly and Kilmarth are privately owned. Please note that the houses are virtually hidden from the view of walkers.

Many locations in Daphne's novels can be visited on foot. You can find Rebecca's cove and the site of Castle Dor; fans of *The House on the Strand* can reconstruct Dick Young's journeys around Tywardreath, and walkers can follow in his footsteps from Chapel Point (about three miles south of Mevagissey) to Bodrugan Barton. The South West Coast Path runs the entire length of Cornwall's spectacular coastline, nearly 300 miles.

Guided walks are held during the Festival and advertised at other times through the tourist information service.

Boat trips from Falmouth will take you up the Helford River to Frenchman's Creek. See www.falriverlinks.co.uk.

Jamaica Inn, a large pub and hotel with a smugglers' theme, lies just off the A30 at Bolventor, midway between Launceston and Bodmin. It has a room devoted to Daphne du Maurier memorabilia, and a shop selling books and videos. See www.jamaicainn.co.uk.

The du Maurier archives, a large collection including notebooks and typescripts, but few personal letters, which can be consulted for research purposes are housed in the Special Collections at the University of Exeter. For access details see www.library.ex.ac.uk/special.

Jeanne du Maurier's paintings can be seen by arrangement at the Royal West of England Academy in Clifton, Bristol (tel. 0117 973 5129). Lectures given at literary events in Cornwall by Alison Oldham offer a rare chance to see slides of Jeanne's work.

The Dartmoor garden created by Jeanne du Maurier and Noël Welch at Half Moon has occasional open days. Contact the National Trust Regional Office in Devon (tel. 01392 881691).

Reading on

Virago has recently reprinted most of Daphne du Maurier's works in attractive new editions with short introductions. See www.virago.co.uk.

Bookends of Fowey specialises in second-hand and antiquarian books on the du Mauriers and other authors associated with Cornwall. See www.bookendsoffowey.com (tel. 01726 833361).

AbeBooks.co.uk gives you easy access to the international market in second-hand books and rare editions.

Inter-library loans are provided by most local libraries.

1 DAPHNE DU MAURIER

The date in brackets gives the year of first publication. The publisher's details show the edition used for page references.

Novels

The Loving Spirit (1931), Virago 2003
I'll Never be Young Again (1932), Virago 2005
Julius (first published as *The Progress of Julius*, 1933), Virago 2004
Jamaica Inn (1936), Virago 2003
Rebecca (1938), Virago 2003
Frenchman's Creek (1941), Virago 2003

Hungry Hill (1943), Gollancz 1943
The King's General (1946), Virago 2004
The Parasites (1949), Virago 2005
My Cousin Rachel (1951), Virago 2003
The Scapegoat (1957), Virago 2004
Castle Dor [with Sir Arthur Quiller-Couch] (1962), Virago 2004
The Glass-Blowers (1963), Virago 2004
The Flight of the Falcon (1965), Virago 2005
The House on the Strand (1969), Virago 2003
Rule Britannia (1972), Virago 2004

Collections of short stories

Come Wind, Come Weather (Heinemann 1940) – uplifting tales for the Moral Rearmament Movement
The Birds and Other Stories (first published as *The Apple Tree*, 1952), Virago 2004
Early Stories (Todd 1955)
The Blue Lenses and Other Stories (first published as *The Breaking Point*, 1959), Penguin 1970
Don't Look Now and Other Stories (first published as *Not After Midnight*, 1971), Penguin 1973 [new Penguin edition 2006]
The Rendezvous and Other Stories (1980), Virago 2005 – includes early stories

Stories discussed in the guide

'The Birds' and 'Monte Verità' first appeared in *The Apple Tree* (1952)
'The Blue Lenses' first appeared in *The Breaking Point* (1959)
'Don't Look Now', 'Not After Midnight', 'A Border-line Case' and 'The Way of the Cross' first appeared in *Not After Midnight* (1971)
'No Motive' first appeared in *The Rendezvous* (1980)
'East Wind' appeared in the US version of *The Rebecca Notebook and Other Memories* (Doubleday 1980). First published in the UK in *Reading Daphne* Truran Books (2007).

Plays

The Years Between (1945)
September Tide (1949)

Non-fiction

Some works are difficult to categorise. For example, *The Glass-Blowers* and *Mary Anne*, included in the following list, are more heavily fictionalised than others.

Gerald: A Portrait (1934), Virago 2004
The Du Mauriers (1937), Virago 2004
The Young George du Maurier: A Selection of His Letters, 1860–67, ed. (Peter Davies 1951)
Mary Anne (1954), Virago 2004
The Glass-Blowers (1963), Virago 2004
Vanishing Cornwall (1967), Penguin 1972 [Virago 2007]
The Infernal World of Branwell Brontë (1960), Virago 2006
Golden Lads: A Study of Anthony Bacon, Francis and Their Friends (1975) [Virago 2007]
The Winding Stair: Francis Bacon, His Rise and Fall (1976), Virago 2006
Myself When Young: The Shaping of a Writer (first published as *Growing Pains*, 1977), Virago 2004
The Rebecca Notebook and Other Memories (1981), Virago 2005

2 ANGELA DU MAURIER (selected books)

Treveryan (1942), Truran 2003
It's Only the Sister: An Autobiography (1951), Truran 2003
The Road to Leenane (1963), Truran 2003
Old Maids Remember, Peter Davies 1966
see www.truranbooks.co.uk

3 BIOGRAPHY AND CRITICISM

Since this guide is designed to focus on Daphne's work rather than her life, what should you read if you want to find out more about the woman as well as the writer?

You might look first to Daphne herself, though she doesn't give enough away. When Daphne composed the brief autobiography of her early life, subtitled *The Shaping of a Writer* (the book's main title, originally *Growing Pains*, was changed to *Myself When Young*), she was not in confessional mode. She provides us with an enjoyable read, but not the insights we are looking for. Writing in her sixties to please her public – and her publishers, as she was still big business – she looks back in amber, casting a sunset glow over the pages. Little is told about the shadowy thoughts that provided the imaginative material for her early writing. And on the social side, her sister Angela does better in *It's Only the Sister*, a lively account of what it was like to be a carefree young woman in the 1920s, and how it felt to spend the war in Fowey – though Angela does not personally do angst, so we get few glimpses into her mental landscape. An article in the *Cornish Review* by Noël Welch, Jeanne du Maurier's companion, provides more subtle insights into the differences between the three talented sisters.

Daphne ends *Myself When Young* with her marriage to Tommy Browning, so we have to read the amusing recollections of her daughter, Flavia Leng, to get any idea of her later family life, and what it was like for her children to grow up in the crumbling house at Menabilly with bats in the roof and a mother musing over her current book. The final lines of *Myself When Young* refer to her departure by boat for her honeymoon on the Helford. She alludes to Frenchman's Creek on the Helford as if her later romantic novel were a tribute to Tommy – indeed she claims as much in an interview recorded for a TV documentary. Since we now know that *Frenchman's Creek* owed more to a wartime affair, our faith in the reliability of this memoir is slightly shaken. Yet the book is, nevertheless, readable and occasionally riveting. Daphne includes extracts from her early diaries that transform the book's texture – oh, those diaries, which du Maurier devotees would kill for, and her family has locked away for fifty years! But we are privileged to have in print absorbing letters covering the difficult period of her double loss of Tommy and Manderley in the correspondence with the younger writer Oriel Malet, published in 1993 with the title *Letters from Menabilly*.

In the same year, Margaret Forster's definitive biography appeared. Since she was commissioned to write it by the du Maurier family after Daphne's death, Forster was given coveted access to private papers which other writers have been denied. Her brilliant book put an end to some of the wilder speculation about Daphne's love life, while replacing it with other carefully researched revelations. It inevitably displaced Judith Cook's earlier biography, published in Daphne's lifetime, which benefited from an interest in the du Mauriers' family history and theatrical background but suffered from a lack of important personal material. Though Forster certainly doesn't tell all, and in some places – by comparison with *Letters from Menabilly*, for example – she stays close to the surface of some psychologically difficult stages in Daphne's life, her book provides us with an extraordinarily frank account of a most fascinating woman.

Biography shortlist

Angela du Maurier, *It's Only the Sister: An Autobiography* (1951), Truran 2003
Noël Welch, 'The Du Mauriers', *Cornish Review*, Summer 1973
Judith Cook, *Daphne: A Portrait of Daphne du Maurier*, Bantam Press 1991
Margaret Forster, *Daphne du Maurier*, Chatto & Windus 1993
Oriel Malet, ed., *Letters from Menabilly: Portrait of a Friendship*, Weidenfeld & Nicholson 1993
Flavia Leng, *Daphne du Maurier: A Daughter's Memoir*, Mainstream 1994

Over the past fifteen years, Daphne's work has attracted serious attention from critics in the universities. Which books are worth trying to get hold of?

The first academic writer to look closely at Daphne's writing was Alison Light, who considered four women writers of the inter-war period in *Forever England* (1991). Daphne might have featured earlier, in the spate of scholarly publications about popular romance that appeared in the 1980s, but in fact only attracted wider critical attention in the context of a turn in university teaching towards Gothic fiction. This specialism produced an excellent book by Avril Horner and Sue Zlosnik on Daphne du Maurier's Gothic imagination (1998). You will find their arguments clear and stimulating, so don't be put off at first by some unfamiliar academic language.

Daphne du Maurier: Haunted Heiress (2000) is written by an American professor, Nina Auerbach, who has produced a rather quirky and unacademic tribute to a favourite author. The book approaches the influence of Daphne's ancestry on her writing from unusual angles. Auerbach is particularly good on the little known novels of George du Maurier and the family's theatrical background. She also examines in some detail the films that male directors have made of Daphne's work.

There is no sign yet of interest in Daphne du Maurier abating, and the centenary will add to the growing pile of publications. Virago is bringing out a diverse collection of writing in *The Daphne du Maurier Companion*, including an interview with the family, the individual introductions to the works that have recently prefaced the new Virago editions, and studies of sequels and adaptations. There is in general a good mix of journalism and scholarship in the thriving industry of Daphne du Maurier criticism, and I hope that readers of Daphne's books who have enjoyed this reader's guide will not hold back from sharing the feast.

Criticism shortlist

Alison Light, *Forever England: Femininity, Literature and Conservatism between the Wars*, Routledge 1991

Avril Horner and Sue Zlosnik, *Daphne du Maurier: Writing, Identity and the Gothic Imagination*, Macmillan 1998

Nina Auerbach, *Daphne du Maurier: Haunted Heiress*, University of Pennsylvania Press 2000

Helen Taylor, ed., *The Daphne du Maurier Companion*, Virago 2007

4 CORNISH CONTEXT

Cornish History

For detailed background to *The King's General*, read the same book as Daphne du Maurier, which remains the standard work on the subject: Mary Coate, *Cornwall in the Great Civil War and Interregnum 1642 – 1660*, Oxford University Press 1933 (reprinted D. Bradford Barton, Truro 1963). See especially chapters 9 and 10 on Sir Richard Grevile and the 1644 Lostwithiel Campaign. For more recent scholarship, see Mark Stoyle, *West Britons: Cornish Identities and the Early Modern British State*, University of Exeter Press 2002.

Philip Payton, *Cornwall*, Alexander Associates 1996, gives an overview of Cornwall's history. For an account of twentieth-century Cornish nationalism, see Bernard Deacon, Dick Cole and Garry Tregidga, *Mebyon Kernow and Cornish Nationalism*, Cardiff, Welsh Academic Press 2003.

Cornish Writing

Writers who have shaped Cornish culture can be insiders or incomers. See Alan Kent, *The Literature of Cornwall: Continuity, Identity, Difference 1000-2000*, Redcliffe Press 2000; Ella Westland, ed. *Cornwall: The Cultural Construction of Place*, Patten Press 1997. Images of Cornwall can of course be shaped from the outside. On the romantic influence, see Simon Trezise, *The West Country as a Literary Invention*, University of Exeter Press 2000, Ella Westland, 'The passionate periphery: Cornwall and romantic fiction' in Ian A. Bell, ed.,*Peripheral Visions*, University of Wales Press 1995.

Index of works discussed

The author

Ella Westland came to Cornwall in 1989, and read *Frenchman' Creek* for the first time since she was a teenager. She was immediately hooked and began thinking more deeply about Daphne du Maurier's work.

During the 1990s she led her first courses on Daphne at Fowey Hotel with the biographer Judith Cook, and teamed up with Lynn Goold for tourist talks and walks. In 1997 she organised a university conference in association with the first Daphne du Maurier Festival.

For many years Ella ran an adult education programme for the University of Exeter in Cornwall. She holds a doctorate from Harvard, and has written on Cornish literature and Victorian culture.

Ella lives with her daughter on the south coast of Cornwall. From the vantage point of the fishermen's cellars at Gorran Haven, where she keeps her dinghy on the slip in summer, she looks across the bay to the Gribben daymark and the cove where Rebecca's boat went down. It was inevitable that some day she would write a book about Daphne du Maurier.

Acknowledgements

This book could not have been written without all those conversations about Daphne du Maurier held over the past fifteen years with friends, colleagues, specialists, students, tourists, festival audiences and reading groups. Warm thanks to local collaborators Bert Biscoe, the late Judith Cook, Helen Doe, Lynn and Bernard Goold, Steph Haxton, John Hurst, Alan Kent, Jo Mattingly, James Whetter, and the Daphne du Maurier Festival team led by Jonathan Aberdeen; to festival speakers including Sally Beauman, Piers Dudgeon, Philippa Gregory, Tony Mott and Justine Picardie; to Ann and David Willmore at *Bookends of Fowey*, and their predecessors, Christine and Howard Alexander; to Bernard Deacon, Philip Payton and Garry Tregidga at the Institute of Cornish Studies; to Avril Horner, Alison Light, Deborah Philips, Helen Taylor, the late Simon Trezise, Gina Wisker and Sue Zlosnick. My debt to earlier writing on du Maurier is considerable, especially Margaret Forster's illuminating biography. At the University of Exeter library, Charlotte Berry, Jessica Gardner and Alasdair Paterson have been unfailingly helpful. Sheila Hodges and Noël Welch have provided telling insights. Alison Oldham has shared her knowledge of Jeanne du Maurier's paintings and kindly contributed a section to this guide. Special thanks are due to Kits and Hacker Browning for their generous hospitality and support. And without the commitment of my publishers, Ivan and Heather Corbett, this book would not, of course, exist.

Ella Westland, Gorran, March 2007